The Philanthropic Revolution

Radical Conservatisms

Elizabeth C. Corey and Patrick J. Deneen, Series Editors

The Philanthropic Revolution

An Alternative History of American Charity

Jeremy Beer

UNIVERSITY OF PENNSYLVANIA PRESS

PHILADELPHIA

Published by
University of Pennsylvania Press
Philadelphia, Pennsylvania 19104–4112

www.upenn.edu/pennpress
Printed in the United States of America

A Cataloging-in-Publication record is
available from the Library of Congress

Cover design by John Hubbard

ISBN 978-0-8122-4793-0 hardcover
ISBN 978-0-8122-9247-3 ebook

Contents

Preface

In this book, I argue that the shift from *charity* to *philanthropy* as the preferred framework for understanding the voluntary use of private resources to benefit others has had surprising—and mostly overlooked—significance. Most fundamentally, this shift has been the result of a reconceptualization of voluntary giving as *primarily a tool for social change*.

Until the nineteenth century, to engage in charity had been for nearly all Americans to affirm, if only implicitly, particular theological claims arising out of traditional Judaism and Christianity. With the rise of philanthropy, the nature of these theological claims changed dramatically. They became bound up with the attempt to assert technological mastery over the social world. Philanthropy has thus served at once as a technique for and a manifestation of revolutionary changes in American life, including secularization, centralization, the bureaucratization of personal relations, and the relative devaluing of locality and place.

I do not argue that charity is religious whereas philanthropy is secular: both are associated with certain theological presuppositions, not only in the most fundamental sense that there is no escaping such presuppositions, but also in the historical sense that philanthropy arises out of a reimagining of Christian eschatology and the proper role of Christianity in society. Nor do I argue that charity is more effective than philanthropy: effectiveness, of course, can only be assessed with respect to specific ends, and with respect to its own fundamentally technological ends, philanthropy is clearly more effective than charity (although perhaps not as effective as its practitioners sometimes claim). Philanthropy's proponents, however, have usually failed to acknowledge that traditional charity's ends are quite different from its own. We are talking about two different things.

I *do* argue that charity is uniquely associated with certain goods—we might call them personalist goods—that are largely unavailable to or tend to be undermined by philanthropy on its own terms, and that insofar as we value those goods, we must look to inject the logic of charity into the modern practice of philanthropy. The halfway-tongue-in-cheek term I assign to this modified, charity-inflected form of philanthropy is *philanthrolocalism*.

In any case, this is an episodic, illustrative, and extremely brief account of why the denigration of charity and the concomitant rise of philanthropy are part of an underappreciated chapter in the American story. My limited goal in this book is to suggest a line of interpretation that has not often been given voice, in the hope that it will prove fruitful to those who carry out more detailed and scholarly investigations.

No one has written more intelligently on modern philanthropy than William Schambra, formerly director of the

Bradley Institute for Philanthropy and Civic Renewal at the Hudson Institute. I do not wish to burden him with my own mistakes and opinions, but it is nonetheless the case that this book is thoroughly permeated by what I have learned from Bill's important writing. Whatever is worthwhile here is due to his influence and example. Along with his many other contributions, Bill directed me to the work of Benjamin Soskis, whose historical insights have significantly shaped my own thinking. One needn't be a very attentive reader to detect that there is little original scholarship contained in these pages, so I would like to express my gratitude to Ben and all the other scholars on whose work this account depends, even as I'm sure they would frequently, perhaps vehemently, disagree with my arguments and conclusions.

I have learned much about the challenges and possibilities presented by contemporary philanthropy from my observations of and conversations with Howard Ahmanson, Wick Allison, Fred Clark, Scott McConnell, George O'Neill Jr., Greg Pfundstein, Tom Riley, and Jon Basil Utley. My colleagues at American Philanthropic and Philanthropy Daily have all provided assistance in various ways throughout this project, especially Jeff Cain, Matt Gerken, and Liz Palla. Damon Linker, my fine editor at the University of Pennsylvania Press, helped shape this book's argument into something approaching coherence. The editors of *Communio* allowed me to reprint some of the text that originally appeared in "Satan Was the First Philanthropist," *Communio* 41 (Fall 2014). And my wife, Kara, patiently listened to my rehearsal of the arguments made herein and helped sharpen my thinking about them. My hearty thanks to all.

What's Missing from the Story of American Philanthropy

> [O]ne of the serious obstacles to the improvement of our race is indiscriminate charity. It were better for mankind that the millions of the rich were thrown into the sea than so spent as to encourage the slothful, the drunken, the unworthy. Of every thousand dollars spent in so-called charity today, it is probable that nine hundred and fifty dollars is unwisely spent—so spent, indeed, as to produce the very evils which it hopes to mitigate or cure.
>
> —Andrew Carnegie[1]

The Western Soup Society was established by an anonymous group of benefactors in Philadelphia in 1837. Its mission, to help relieve the plight of the poor, was simple, and its method, the establishment of a soup kitchen on Philadelphia's west side, just as basic. Fifteen thousand quarts of soup were ladled out to all comers—local or transient, black or white—during the winter of 1837–38. Potatoes and rice were added to the menu in 1842, and in 1845 a local philanthropist named Paul Beck left the society a substantial bequest that allowed it to expand further its service to the poor, including the addition of a lunch program for black students at a nearby school.[2]

Except, perhaps, for its precociously interracial nature, there was little about the society's charitable work that was atypical for its time. Thousands of soup kitchens and similar "outdoor relief" programs operated in cities and towns across America in the first half of the nineteenth century, brought into being not only by the severe dislocations produced by a burgeoning industrial economy but also by Americans' relatively newfound enthusiasm for the establishment of voluntary, nongovernmental associations aimed at helping those in need.

Yet by the 1830s and 1840s, such associations increasingly found themselves the targets of criticism. Critics accused groups like the Western Soup Society of encouraging idleness and vice by indiscriminately feeding the unworthy and the lazy. These critics wished to eliminate the sort of "outdoor relief" practiced by the Western Soup Societies of the nation and to replace it with almshouses, workhouses, and asylums: so-called *indoor* relief. In these kinds of institutions, the poor could be taught discipline and work habits. And the idle, being forced to live in and abide by the rules of such institutions, which were not often pleasant, would be discouraged from seeking relief and encouraged to make themselves socially useful.

Lurking behind these criticisms was the notion that poor relief must be judged first and foremost by its consequences. This may seem like an obvious, even commonsense view of the matter today, but it actually represented a dramatic conceptual shift. For centuries, even millennia, the voluntary giving of one's goods and time in the service of others was in Western culture associated with and justified as an expression of biblical charity. Charity embodied an inescapably personalist and remarkably nonconsequentialist ethic. In the increasingly sophisticated world of the nineteenth century, it looked more and more like a scandal to progressive thinkers.

"The poor you will always have with you," the Gospel of Matthew reports Jesus as having said to his followers. By the mid- to late 1800s, the new critics of charity were daring to think he was wrong. Poverty and other social ills could ultimately be eliminated, perhaps through the application of the right social policies; at the very least, they needn't be perpetuated by unthinkingly rewarding sloth or immorality. In short, the founders of the Western Soup Society, not to mention their patrons, thought it their obligation to feed the poor among them. The critics thought it more important to try to discourage, if not end, poverty altogether.

Within a few decades, philanthropists such as Andrew Carnegie and John D. Rockefeller, having amassed stunningly large fortunes, would side decisively with traditional charity's critics. The logic of technology—a logic we now take for granted so much that we might be said to inhabit it—was on their side. By adopting this logic, the new, scientific practitioners of voluntary giving, eventually known as philanthropists, would use their wealth to achieve great victories: the virtual abolition of certain diseases, massive increases in agricultural yields, and advancement of basic and applied research in numerous fields. And by adopting this logic, they would advance causes that might be viewed more skeptically, including eugenics and forced sterilization, the secularization and centralization of American society, and the idea that the fates of individual places and the loving care of particular persons are secondary considerations.

Despite the purported conservatism of men like Carnegie and Rockefeller, in both its rhetoric and in its practice, modern philanthropy was revolutionary.

For most Americans, contemporary philanthropy seems "revolutionary" only in the sense that it has been wildly successful. After all, few aspects of contemporary American life are more widely and effusively praised than American philanthropy. In popular treatments—and in more than a few academic ones as well—the American philanthropic tradition is treated as an uncomplicated story of achievement.

The sheer scale of philanthropy in America is astonishing. As of 2012, there were more than 86,000 active private foundations in the United States, controlling approximately $715 billion in assets. These foundations disbursed a record $52 billion,[3] which seems like a lot, until one realizes that it is a relatively small proportion of the entire giving pie, which totaled $335 billion in 2013.[4] The bulk of American giving ($241 billion in 2013) is driven by individuals. The impulse to give is hardly restricted to the wealthy—the poor give away a much higher percentage of their disposable income than do the rich—and the menu of America's charitable options is almost endless. All told, approximately two-thirds of American households give each year to one or more of the *1.44 million* charities that they and their fellows are constantly forming.[5]

Put in global context, these are impressive numbers. American voluntary giving is approximately equal to the entire gross domestic product (GDP) of Denmark. The $715 billion in assets controlled by US foundations—money that is of course invested in the US economy in various ways—is larger than the Swiss economy, which is the twentieth largest in the world. Arthur Brooks, after analyzing what little comparative international data there are on private giving and accounting for differences in living standards, concluded that Americans "gave more than twice as much of their incomes to charity as the Dutch, almost three times as much as the French, more than five times as much as the Germans, and ten times as much as the Italians."[6] Another study found that the value of American philanthropy, according to the standard national accounts data system, is equivalent to 5.5 percent of the national GDP—the highest in the world, by far (in no other country did it equal even 2 percent of GDP).[7]

The metrics, in other words, suggest that voluntary giving is of surpassing importance to Americans, a conclusion that is confirmed by the fact that philanthropists are among our most celebrated heroes. To be a successful entrepreneur, politician, or entertainer is to win a place of high regard in most American hearts—think of Bill Gates, Bill Clinton, and Oprah Winfrey. Then consider how much *more* highly thought of the two Bills and Oprah became after they turned their focus to philanthropy. We like our tablets, humming economies, and celebrity chats. But even twenty-first-century Americans realize that providing the citizens of the world's poorer countries with vaccinations, disaster-recovery assistance, and model schools are more noble endeavors, and we are quick to honor them.

Nor is there any indication that America's wealthiest men and women are retreating from philanthropy. The

Giving Pledge, cofounded by Gates and Warren Buffett in 2010, encourages America's billionaires to commit to giving away at least 50 percent of their wealth during their lifetimes or upon their death. As of November 2014, the Pledge had 127 signatories—nearly 8 percent of the world's 1,645 billionaires.

In sum, Americans voluntarily give away a lot of money; they are probably more generous than any of the world's other peoples; and American giving is a multifarious, diverse, top-to-bottom affair. No wonder that the story of American philanthropy is usually narrated as it is.

Yet despite their frequent celebrations of the health of American philanthropy, many representatives of today's philanthropy establishment are troubled by the way Americans give. Despite well over a century of concerted effort to educate Americans on how to be more effective in their giving, American philanthropy, they argue, is still not strategic enough. It is irrational, wasteful, parochial, and politically backward.

For example, for the past two decades or so, the "strategic philanthropy" movement has attempted—with some success—to get foundations to require their grantees to rigorously measure the impact of their work so that funders can direct their giving according to meaningful metrics. Yet according to one estimate, "*only 3 percent* of donors give based on the relative performance of charities," much to the chagrin of the philanthropy establishment.[8]

Inspired in part by the work of the controversial Princeton ethicist Peter Singer, the partisans of "effective altruism" extend the basic principle of strategic

philanthropy by arguing that givers have a moral obligation not only to be *effective* with their giving but also to
direct their giving to wherever it will do the most good—
to "save or improve the most lives per dollar, no matter what
a program does or where it's located."[9] Utilitarian considerations are, in the view of the effective altruists, the only ones
that should drive giving; geographic propinquity, loyalty,
kinship, and other such factors must be ignored. Yet almost
no one except a few zealots and cutting-edge foundations
actually practices this kind of giving.

The National Committee on Responsive Philanthropy
(NCRP), for its part, argues that foundations and philanthropists give far too much to causes and cultural institutions that are primarily of interest to the middle class and
wealthy and not enough to systemic efforts to fight poverty and bring about a more diverse and inclusive society.
American giving, in other words, is too often reactionary
where it ought to be radical. Yet to this point, at least, the
NCRP's efforts have apparently made little headway in
transforming the giving practices of nonelite donors and
philanthropic institutions.

What is going on here? Although it is rarely articulated
in such fashion, we might summarize these complaints by
saying that today's philanthropy establishment is troubled
by the extent to which American giving continues to be
guided by the logic of charity rather than philanthropy.

This is a very old complaint, one that has been regu-
larly leveled against Americans since the term *philanthropy*
gradually came into use on these shores in the mid- to late
nineteenth century. In the century or so prior, the word
was typically used in a somewhat different yet tellingly
related way: as a synonym for *benevolent* or *humanitarian*.

To be a philanthropist was to love humanity as a whole, which is to say in the abstract, and to be engaged in or at least sympathetic to various, sometimes self-consciously secular, reform schemes. Philanthropy was very different from traditional charity, and its rise was therefore controversial and contested.

Today, most people, if asked to reflect on the difference between philanthropy and charity, would likely answer that philanthropy is charity writ large—charity as it is practiced by the wealthy and/or by professionals. But as we will see in examining its distinctive origins, history, and features, philanthropy is not simply charity brought to scale. It is not simply institutionalized or even professionalized charity. From a theoretical standpoint, the most important difference between philanthropy and charity— the truly revolutionary difference—is that the logic of philanthropy invites us to see voluntary giving within a primarily *technological* and *global* rather than *theological* and *local* framework.[10]

For more than one hundred years, philanthropy has been viewed by most of its influential practitioners as a tool for rationalizing society—as a tool for overcoming and eroding the barriers posed by traditional religion, by local practices and institutions, and by decentralized government to certain notions of reform and progress. This modern view of philanthropy as essentially a social technology spearheaded by private elites stands in contrast to both the civic perspective of *philanthropia* held by the ancient Romans, wherein voluntary giving served as a way for the wealthy and the local populace to affirm their mutual ties by honoring one another, and the Jewish and Christian perspective of charity, wherein voluntary giving serves as a grave religious duty and privileged means of drawing closer to God. Although the early Christian church resolutely opposed its teaching on caritas to the pagan practice of philanthropia (and vice versa), both caritas and philanthropia were practices highly conditioned by considerations of both theology and place.

In short, however successful—or unsuccessful— philanthropy has been in curing disease, reforming social relations, improving agricultural yields, or addressing any other specific area on which it has fixed its gaze, its revolutionary character is most accurately reflected in the degree to which it has succeeded and continues to succeed in changing the way many people, and especially elites, think about the purposes and possibilities of voluntary giving.

To its critics, the consequences of this philanthropic turn have been mixed—much more mixed, in any case, than is typically conceded. For example, although we still do not know as much as we should about the topic, and foundations themselves have been loath to highlight it, the American philanthropy establishment played a central role in the early twentieth-century eugenics movement, including bankrolling the forced sterilization of tens of thousands of Americans.

The philanthropic way of thinking also leads to what seem to be absurdities. When a spokeswoman for the $37 billion Bill and Melinda Gates Foundation was asked why the foundation chose not to assist dozens of homeless sleeping outside its $500 million Seattle headquarters, despite having made the issue of homelessness one of its focus areas, she replied, "We're trying to move upstream to a systems level to either prevent family homelessness before it happens or to end it as soon as possible after it happens."[11] Similarly, Warren Buffett's son Howard Buffett recently told an interviewer that he had gotten a "sinking feeling" after visiting a village in Africa and being begged by a mother to help care for her sick child, since he realized that while he could have saved the life of that baby and many others, upon running the numbers it simply wouldn't have been strategic to pursue such a course. "That was a hard lesson to learn," he added.[12] No doubt the child's mother felt the same way.

There are at least three major scholarly perspectives on the development of American philanthropy. The first—the most culturally if not the most academically dominant— is the Whig perspective given especially pure voice by the historian Olivier Zunz in his book *Philanthropy in America*.[13] This perspective tells the story of philanthropy as one of unadulterated progress and unquestionable goodwill. It is the story preferred by—and therefore unceasingly retailed by—the great philanthropic foundations themselves.

The second perspective is one preferred by leftish scholars influenced by Marxist, Foucauldian, and/or class-centered analyses. It emphasizes the way charity and later philanthropy have acted as systems of social control intended to maintain class boundaries and serve middle-class and elite interests.[14] There is much to this sort of analysis, I believe, and I freely make use of it. But like the Whig narrative, it is far from the whole story.

The third perspective tends to be preferred by liberal scholars of the consensus school. They are not as inclined as the Whigs to give philanthropy's protagonists a free pass and not as inclined as the leftish scholars to see philanthropy as only, or primarily, a tool of class interests. Rather, they tend to view the rise of "scientific charity" and philanthropy as leading, happily, to the advancement of the American welfare state, such as it is. The representatives of philanthropy, scientific charity, social work, and social reform generally are therefore seen as paving the way toward a necessary safety net, even if they often betrayed class biases and had less than pure motives. This perspective is more balanced than the first two, perhaps, but its uncritical embrace of the welfare state and its champions is not entirely illuminating.[15]

Of course, many scholars draw from more than one of these perspectives in their work. But surprisingly few draw from the alternative view of philanthropy I sketch here, which owes more to theologically grounded critiques of liberalism, centralized bureaucracy, and the ideology of progress than the aforementioned schools of thought.[16] This perspective rests on the premise that the marginalization of the discourse of charity for that of philanthropy is part of a dominant Enlightenment narrative, one that has opportunistically "invented a dichotomy between the religious and the secular and constructed the former as an irrational and dangerous impulse that must give way in public to rational, secular forms of power." What counts as "religion," or an aspect thereof, William Cavanaugh argues, is the result "of a particular configuration of power, that of the modern, liberal nation-state as it developed in the West."[17]

Cavanaugh claims that prior to the 1940s, religion was generally seen as a unitive force in American life and that only after that time did it gradually become regarded as essentially divisive. It might be more correct to say, however, that a very certain kind of religion—mainline Protestantism—was seen as unitive in pre–World War II America and that other religions, including Catholicism and Judaism, were seen as unitive only insofar as they did not publicly emphasize those ecclesial claims and practices that clashed with mainline Protestantism—and only insofar as they very publicly manifested their commitment to the American project as that project was understood by mainline American Protestants.

Philanthropy's most vocal proponents quite clearly regarded certain manifestations of religion as divisive from the very beginning of the benevolence revolution in the 1830s. Anti-Catholicism was one of the prime moving forces behind many of the first voluntary associations; the family practices, poverty, and alien immigrant mores of Catholics and Jews spurred further development of America's philanthropic associations among all sects (including Catholics and Jews) in the middle to late 1800s; and a religious-versus-secular discourse emerged with respect to government's proper role in the realm of charity by the second half of the nineteenth century. In this discourse, Catholics, Jews, and Mormons were improperly religious or "sectarian," and they were certainly irrational and fanatical. Mainline Protestants, Unitarians, and unbelieving pragmatists and humanists, on the other hand, had a respect for the integrity of the secular sphere that made true progress possible. The particular (and unavoidable) theological assumptions, beliefs, and prejudices of these latter groups therefore went largely unexamined as the philanthropic revolution took its triumphant course.

The following counterhistory, in contrast, takes seriously—and therefore foregrounds—the experiences and ideas of some of those who questioned or resisted the rise of scientific charity and the new philanthropy, including especially representatives of Jewish, Christian, and ethnic communities. It is somewhat strange that, even from a purely historical perspective, theological considerations play such a minor role in both the historiography of giving and the discourse of contemporary philanthropy. After all, philanthropia was a significant aspect of Roman religious piety, and charity is one of the three theological virtues in traditional Christian thought and central to the Jewish tradition. Even in their secular forms, the charitable institutions and practices characteristic of modern America—indeed the world—are unimaginable absent the influences of Judaism and Christianity.

More specifically, throughout American history, men, women, and institutions have frequently if not usually understood their acts of charity in the terms of a particular theological framework. That framework and the changes it has undergone are largely missing from the story of American philanthropy told by conservative Whigs, leftists, and liberals alike.

In chapter 1, I review the biblical roots of American charity. How did the Jewish and Christian thinkers and communities of late antiquity conceptualize the voluntary giving of their goods and selves, and how was this different from the conception embedded within the surrounding culture? To understand how the logic of charity differs from the logic of philanthropy, we need to go back and see what made charity such a radical concept in the first place.

Chapter 2 sketches the course of charitable thinking in America from the colonial period until the Civil War. The earliest European settlers inherited a view of charity that was largely—but not entirely—in keeping with the traditional view that reigned in Europe for more than a thousand years. The Enlightenment, new social conditions wrought by the Industrial Revolution, and the new way of seeing the world embedded within and taught by new technologies conspired to make the traditional view of charity less persuasive to many. The Second Great Awakening, which peaked in the 1820s and 1830s, taught many evangelical Christians to see their faith as requiring them to work for the salvation of the world through various kinds of social reform. It contributed significantly to the devaluing of traditional charity in the eyes of Christians themselves.

In chapter 3, which covers the years between the Civil War and the Great Depression, the philanthropic revolution fully arrives. The partisans of "scientific charity" and the practitioners of the new philanthropy ceaselessly criticize and ridicule the practices and worldview associated with traditional charity. The story usually ends there. But we see that the thinkers and communities who still adhered to charity—primarily Jews, Catholics, less assimilated ethnic groups, and America's mutual-aid fraternal orders—had cogent responses, responses that gain force when we view them within the context of the new philanthropy's most daring social experiment: eugenics.

Finally, chapter 4 suggests how in the twentieth century, the community foundation and settlement house movements to some degree held traditional charity in tension with the demands of professional philanthropy.

Outside the establishment, figures such as Dorothy Day demonstrated the ethical appeal and power of a more radical devotion to charity, while James C. Scott's account of twentieth-century "high modernism" is used to indicate the epistemic limits of Big Philanthropy.

Finally, to the extent that one admits that certain goods are lost in the turn away from charity, how might those goods be retrieved in a way that also does justice to the evident goods associated with philanthropy? The last part of chapter 4 posits some potential answers to that question by advocating for a new "philanthrolocalism" that takes places and persons seriously as ends in themselves.

Chapter 1

Unlocking the Universe's Secret

The Theological Roots of American Charity

> Not only were the ideal recipients of the Christian gift—
> the poor—different from the traditional recipients of urban
> benefactions—the citizens, many of whom were by no means
> poor—but the imagined effects of giving were also profoundly
> different. Behind the Christian notion of giving to the poor
> lay the novel idea that giving to the poor (and to other pious
> causes) involved a transfer of wealth from this world to the next,
> summed up in the notion of placing *treasure in heaven.*
>
> —Peter Brown[1]

The story of charity in America is a fundamentally Jewish and Christian story. The way that Americans have thought about voluntary giving has been from the beginning decisively shaped by the biblical tradition that has played such a large role in forming American thinking, society, and culture. The practice of charity was, and is, central to that tradition. Thus to understand what was at stake in the critique of charity mounted by the partisans of philanthropy in the modern period, we must first examine what was at stake in the attack on pagan philanthropia by the partisans of Christian caritas in late antiquity. In other words, before there was a philanthropic revolution, there was a charitable one.

In the Greco-Roman world of late antiquity—let us say the 100–400 AD period—"most persons lived miserable lives, at a standard of living that never reached beyond that enjoyed by the populations of other pre-industrial empires," in the words of Peter Brown. Yet persons in need could find assistance only through one of three primary sources: the family, patronage, and philanthropy. For many people—especially the truly poor, the sick, the widowed, and the orphaned—these sources of help were often inaccessible.

Roman patrons, for example, did not enter into patronage relationships with the truly needy. Their clients had to be socially respectable, for they had to be able to give something in return—"votes, money, or prestige"— for their patrons' assistance. That assistance was by no means characterized by selflessness. As one scholar states, "The patronage system offered much more incentive for the exploitation of clients than for their care."[2]

The practice of philanthropy (philanthropia) by the wealthy did redound to the benefit of the needy, and on occasion private citizens provided goods such as grain, oil, and money to the general public. But these benefits were neither regular nor reliable, and their intent was not to ease the suffering of the worst-off but to augment their donors' reputation for piety. Philanthropia was therefore not surprisingly often practiced during religious festivals, and it was targeted toward the general citizenry—if the most needy received a share of this largesse, that was at best a happy accident.[3] Philanthropia was intended to be conspicuous and, as with patronage, to increase the giver's honor, prestige, or political capital.[4]

In the interest of political stability, the Roman empire's governmental bodies sometimes gave food and other kinds of material aid to the poor, but "even this aid was only intended for the relatively poor, the *penes*, and not for the truly destitute, *ptochos*. Indeed, provision of any sort of aid to the truly destitute, beggars, was considered contemptible; it only encouraged them."[5] As a popular dictum of the dramatist Plautus (254–184 BC) went, "He does the beggar a bad service who gives him meat and drink, for what he gives is lost, and the life of the poor is prolonged to their own misery." In the face of such views, reported St. John Chrysostom (347–407) in the fourth century AD, beggars sometimes tried to "earn" donations by entertaining prospective givers with "tricks" such as "eating the leather from worn out shoes," "driving sharp nails into their heads," and "plunging their naked bodies in water frozen by the cold."[6]

The extended family was the most important and by far the most frequently called-upon source of aid in late antiquity. But family could not always be relied upon. Plague or illness might wipe out a good portion of one's relatives—and hence one's support system. Then, too, "it was by no means unheard of that the chronically ill might be shunned, having become too great an economic burden or too extreme a risk of contagion for a family teetering at the edge of mere survival," writes Andrew Crislip. He suggests that this may have been what had happened to those lepers mentioned in Luke's Gospel who, living on the edge of town, called out to Jesus for mercy.[7]

The elderly were sometimes abandoned, and the threat of eventual abandonment was a cause of much anxiety. Slaves had it worse. They were "commonly cast out when no longer profitable, left for dead in the agora or temple." If they survived, they might have the misfortune of out-living their own children and relatives and thus when old would again find no help available to them.[8] No provision of shelter was made by Roman institutions at all for the poor, and health care was generally unavailable to them outside the family, except for the occasional charitable physician (although "the clever physician would refuse any patient unlikely to recover, thus enhancing his rate of success").[9] In sum, "whether in health care, shelter, food, or clothing, those with limited or no recourse to family were quickly reduced to a usually short life of itinerant beggary."[10]

In directing their patronage toward clients who could help them; in ensuring that their philanthropy was vis-ible and directed toward the public at large; and in mak-ing relatively little effort to succor the poor, sick, elderly, and enslaved, the ancient Greeks and Romans were not acting impiously. After all, no god of the Greco-Roman world demanded that one show charity toward the needy. Their suffering was of little if any interest to these deities, and therefore helping them was not a religious obligation. The theologian Gary Anderson emphasizes that when rich Romans did make donations to assist the less fortunate, such donations were not regarded as serving a religious function.[11]

We must be careful to add a number of qualifications to this story, for voluntary giving was far from unknown in the ancient Mediterranean world. The Roman lower classes, for example, often formed benefit societies that provided financial and material aid to their members, including food and burial funds.[12] The institution of patronage, even if it was self-interested and exploitative, often helped get people through hard times or back on their feet. And the wealthy sincerely valued and honored the magnanimous giving away of wealth. Roman sarcophagi often featured the *chriophoros*, a symbol of philanthropy that consisted of a carved relief of a man carrying a sheep on his shoulder. The chriophoros was often paired with the *orans*, a hand uplifted in prayer. "The two figures represent the two chief characteristics of a virtuous man or woman, piety and respect toward the gods and philanthropy and justice toward one's fellow human beings."[13]

Furthermore, not unlike contemporary American elites, the Roman rich generously supported cultural institutions and the general welfare, and they liked to be recognized for that generosity. An extant inscription notes that Pliny the Younger (61–113 AD), a high-ranking government official, "left by will public baths . . . and an additional 300,000 sesterces for furnishing them, with interest on 200,000 for their upkeep . . . and also to his city capital of 1,866,666 2/3 sesterces to support a hundred of his freedman, and subsequently to provide an annual dinner for the people of the city. . . . Likewise in his lifetime he gave 500,000 sesterces for the maintenance of boys and girls of the city, and also 100,000 for the upkeep of the library."[14] There is no reason to think that Pliny's generosity was unusual among his class. Philanthropy as an aspect of religious piety was so integral to the Roman way of life that the Christian apologist Tertullian emphasized it as a point of connection between paganism and Christianity.[15]

Yet it is nevertheless true that the sensibilities and practices associated with Roman philanthropia on the one hand and biblical caritas on the other were strikingly different. Unlike their Roman counterparts, Jews and Christians were so uniquely dedicated to serving the sick, impoverished, and unwanted that a number of new Latin and Greek words had to be invented to name the institutions they created for this purpose. Why this difference? A number of theories have been put forward, but the simplest is still the most persuasive: for Jews and Christians, charity was *salvific*. For them, to give generously from one's wealth to the needy was not merely an act of civic piety; it was to "lay up treasure in heaven," and thus it had the deepest and most lasting personal significance possible.

Charitable deeds were central to the theology of late-antique Judaism. For example, *mitsva*, the Hebrew word for commandment, has a secondary meaning of "charity." As one rabbinic text explains, "Giving alms is equal to keeping all the commandments in the Torah."[16] Moses himself made clear the Jew's obligation to those in need:

> If there is among you anyone in need, a member of your community in any of your towns within the land that the Lord your God is giving you, do not be hard-hearted or tight-fisted toward your needy neighbor. You should rather open your hand, willingly lending enough to meet the need, whatever it may be. . . . Give liberally and be ungrudging when you do so, for on this account the Lord your God will bless you in all your work and in all that you undertake. Since there will never cease to be some in need on the earth, I therefore command you, "Open your hand to the poor and needy neighbor in your land." (Deut. 15:7–11)

For Jews and their early Christian counterparts alike, to give to the needy was truly to lay up treasure in heaven. Gary Anderson argues that three proverbs were central to the growth of a distinctive biblical theology of almsgiving that held that to give to the poor is to make deposits in a heavenly treasury. The first of these, Proverbs 10:2, reads, "The treasuries of wickedness provide no benefit, but almsgiving delivers from death." The second, Proverbs 11:4, reads, "Riches provide no benefit on the day of wrath, but almsgiving delivers from death." And the third, Proverbs 19:17, reads, "Whoever is kind to the poor lends to the Lord, and will be repaid in full."

Thus, for example, for the Jewish author of Sirach, Ben Sira, "the money expended as charity returns to the donor as a credit to a heavenly bank account."[17] Sirach shows that "having money is tantamount to a spiritual ordeal whose outcome is determined by whether one has the courage to give it away."[18] The Book of Tobit also reveals the influence of these key Proverbs. Tobit says to his son Tobias, "Do not turn your face away from anyone who is poor, and the face of God will not be turned away from you. If you have many possessions, make your gift from them in proportion; if few, do not be afraid to give according to the little you have. So you will be laying up a good treasure for yourself against the day of necessity. For almsgiving delivers from death and keeps you from going into the darkness." Anderson notes that it is because of the pervasiveness of this view of almsgiving that Jewish beggars would say the phrase "*zeki bi*"—"acquire a merit through me"—when asking for money.[19]

Christ intensified the Jewish teaching concerning the poor. He references the special status of almsgiving in Mark 10:21, when he tells the rich young man who wishes to follow him to "go sell what you own, and give the money to the poor, and you will have treasure in heaven." In Matthew 6, Jesus states that prayer, fasting, and almsgiving are together the means by which a person stores currency in the heavenly treasury. In Matthew 25, he develops this teaching further, instructing his disciples that he is himself present in the needy and that when one ministers to them, one therefore serves him as well: "For I was hungry and you gave me food, I was thirsty and you gave me drink, I was a stranger and you welcomed me, I was naked and you clothed me, I was sick and you visited me, I was in prison and you came to me." The church would eventually come to refer to these acts as the corporal works of mercy.

This high view of almsgiving is present in stories of the early apostles, as well. Tabitha, the woman St. Peter raises from the dead in Acts 9, is described as a woman "devoted to good works and acts of charity." The story notes that the beneficiaries of her charity are there with her, mourning, when Peter arrives. Surely, Anderson argues, this detail is meant to signify the salvific consequences of her life of giving.

In short, charity is absolutely central to the biblical theology that informed the development of both the Jewish and Christian traditions in the ancient world. The early church provides further evidence. St. Basil of Caeserea (329–79), continuing to develop the orthodox teaching, argued that to help the poor is to make a gift as well as a loan. It is a loan in that God pays back the giver. And God does this because he is himself incarnate in the poor man.

The special and very real presence of God in the poor was widely emphasized by the church fathers. St. John Chrysostom (347–407) preached, "Whenever . . . you see a poor believer, imagine that you behold an altar. Whenever you meet a beggar, don't insult him, but reverence him." Pope Leo the Great (400–461) held that almsgiving is "so important that, though the other virtues exist without it, they can be of no avail. For although a person be full of faith, and chaste, and sober, and adorned with other still greater decorations, yet if he is not merciful, he cannot deserve mercy."

Christian practice by and large matched the theory. The Roman emperor Julian the Apostate (330–63), who struggled to restore the old Roman cult after his uncle Constantine had made Christianity the official religion of the empire, grudgingly paid tribute to the central, and utterly unique, place of charity in Jewish and Christian practice. He believed that it was the new religion's revolutionary practices of feeding the poor and ministering to the sick that was gaining it converts, so he ordered his priests to copy these acts in order that the traditional religion might better compete with its Christian rival. It was Christians' "benevolence to strangers, their care for the graves of the dead and the pretended holiness of their lives" that had led to the growth of the church, wrote Julian to Arsacius, high priest of Galatia. He went on to lament that "the impious Galilaeans support not only their own poor but ours as well; all men see that our people lack aid from us."[20]

The eminent historian of antiquity Peter Brown agrees that almsgiving was central not only to Christian theology but also to Christian practice during the late Roman period. "Long before the conversion of Constantine, the Christian care of the poor had been impressive," he writes.[21] Brown notes that by the year 251, the bishop of Rome claimed that he was providing financial support to 1,500 widows and other needy persons. Early bishops certainly deployed Christian giving to help grow the church and to put it in a more secure political position. And as with pagan philanthropy, the building and furnishing of churches provided occasions for the wealthy to demonstrate their piety—and to be recognized for it. Yet when Jewish and Christian donors "gave, they made clear that they gave also—indeed, primarily—to god."[22]

No matter how important its acts of charity may have been in winning adherents, the early Christian church did not view these acts first through a utilitarian lens. Charity was not a means, at least not primarily, of solving a social problem, redistributing wealth, or even growing the church.[23] To practice charity was to make a statement about the world and the God who had created and redeemed it. To engage in charity was to give "testimony to the love of God inscribed in the natural order" by imitating and witnessing to his mercy.[24] Almsgiving was closely linked with the Eucharist in the minds of early Christians: one gave of oneself, in the former, in order to imitate God's total self-giving in the latter. As Anderson puts it, in the traditional biblical conception, "the believer recognizes himself in a world that rewards charity because it was founded upon charity. . . . Funding a treasury becomes a rational act for the believer because by acting this way she is actually swimming with the current that God has fixed in the created order. This is why the one who gives away her money becomes the most effective saver for the future. The emphasis is not on my own self-interest but on unlocking a secret about the structure of the universe."[25]

We start to see why the Greco-Roman world regarded the Christians as so radical. Their claims about the nature of the world and the divine were shocking, and their devotion to the needy no less so.

Thanks to the centrality of charity in the burgeoning new Christian cult, from the fourth century until the dawn of the Reformation in the early sixteenth century, a new network of charitable institutions was born and brought to maturity. One such entity, the *diaconia*, a monastic institution responsible for works of charity, had developed in Egypt by the middle of the fourth century. By the sixth century, it had juridical status, and before long each diocese had its own diaconia (Rome itself had a diaconia by the seventh or eighth century).[26]

A Roman noblewoman, St. Fabiola, started the first hospital in the Western world in 399, personally ministering to patients there. Hospitals were even more prevalent and advanced in Eastern Christendom until the high Middle Ages, when a dynamic hospital movement took form. The Benedictines themselves founded more than two thousand hospitals, and beginning in 1099 the Knights Hospitallers were also especially active in this movement, founding hospitals, hospices, almshouses, shelters for the poor, food kitchens, and orphanages throughout Europe and the Holy Land.[27]

Numerous other religious orders dedicated themselves to succoring the sick, the disabled, widows, and orphans as the Middle Ages passed. Voluntary confraternities or guilds looked after needy members and founded hospitals and orphanages. Churches provided food and money to those in need. The wealthy provided funds for the building and decoration of churches and other institutions (e.g., the building and repair of bridges), and in their wills they left funds for feeding the poor or even for paying villages' tax bills. At the dawn of the Reformation, charitable institutions and practices had reached a high level of maturity within Christendom,[28] and they continued to develop at a robust pace even after the rupture of the church.

Ettore Vernazza, for example, founded a devotional confraternity called the Oratory in Genoa in 1497 for both laypersons and those consecrated to religious vocations. Its twin pillars—devotion to the Eucharist and caring for the sick, especially those suffering from syphilis— reflect the close relationship that persisted in the Catholic mind between the encounter with Christ under the species of bread and the encounter with him under the species of the needy. During the sixteenth century, and especially once the Counter-Reformation was well under way, Catholics if anything "renewed their commitment to relieving the distress of the poor," in the words of Reformation historian Diarmaid MacCulloch. New orders such as the Ursulines, founded by Angela Merici in 1535, combined teaching the poor with charitable works. The Sisters of Charity of St. Vincent de Paul "organized education alike for rich and poor girls, ran soup-kitchens for the desperate, nursed in hospitals and even undertook work in parishes under the direction of parish clergy."

The Counter-Reformation-inspired Daughters of Charity made it their vocation "to imitate Christ by assisting the poor and to serve the Church by keeping the poor from heresy. Thus, political and social considerations were inseparable from religious and spiritual ones," and "many other religious communities of women dedicated to nursing and teaching . . . imitated their example."[29] Charity was also provided through private associations of laymen, which flowered in Catholic countries during the Counter-Reformation. In Milan, by 1600, one in three to four adult males belonged to a confraternity, as did many women and adolescents. Guild activities that had been disrupted or destroyed during the Reformation period were often renewed by religious orders such as the Jesuits.

In all this activity, the theology of charity remained explicit and paramount: by giving to those in need, one gave to Christ himself, thereby laying up treasure in heaven. The works of mercy had salvific merit. That was the principle reason one ought to give one's time and money to others.

There were, of course, other reasons for Catholic leaders to engage in and encourage charity. As in ancient Rome, the poor had in part to be cared for simply in order to maintain public order. And voluntary giving on a large scale surely resulted in public honor—no small incentive to give. But these reasons for charitable activity were well integrated into the larger theology of charity (e.g., good public order was part of God's will, and to be honored publicly for one's gifts ensured that one would be prayed for by those whom one's gift helped). There was as yet no thought that voluntary giving might be seen primarily as a tool by which to fundamentally transform the social order or permanently ameliorate human suffering, let alone as an activity without explicit religious import.

The Reformation changed things—but not as much as one might suspect. Its principal effect was to intensify certain trends that had begun earlier. Thus since at least the twelfth century, theologians and canon lawyers had debated whether and how to distinguish between the unworthy and the worthy poor. Authorities in Reformed territories may have emphasized the importance of this distinction, but they didn't introduce it. Efforts to improve the efficiency of poor relief had also begun well before the Reformation, as had, in some territories, the delivery of such relief by civil rather than ecclesiastical authorities.

After the Reformation, and especially but not exclusively in Protestant territories, the focus on efficiency and the avoidance of redundancy seems to have become more intense, and the civil authorities certainly tended to become more involved in providing care to the poor and needy. But we should not exaggerate these differences, as these basic trends not only were in place prior to the Reformation but afterwards took place in many Catholic territories as well. (In part, this was because poverty in the fifteenth century had become intensified thanks to economic factors.) Thomas Max Safley emphasizes that although the early modern period saw the growing centralization and secularization of charity measures, these trends did not eradicate the traditional Christian view, and in many places charity remained under local and ecclesial control. "For the sixteenth-century laity, . . . poor relief remained linked to ideas of interior, individual salvation."[30]

Finally, for the Reformers, no less than for their Catholic rivals, acts of charity were seen through an explicitly and intensely theological lens. Charity was still preached and thought of as a Christian duty within Protestant communities. The Christian was still called upon to imitate Christ in the giving of his or her self (and by extension property) to others. And to engage in charitable acts could also be seen as a manifestation of grace in the "saved" Christian's life—a sign of one's election and redemption. That was no small thing. Then, too, old religious habits did not change overnight. Even among Protestants, it was common for wills to include a generous gift for the poor, including food and drink for the very needy.

Yet the Reformers' theology of charity was also fundamentally different from that of Catholics, thanks to their insistence that works had no salvific merit whatsoever. As we have seen, in the sacramental theology of the Catholic Church, charity was, like the Eucharist, a special conduit of grace for those who engaged in it, and thus the objects of charity—beggars, the poor, the widowed and orphaned—acquired special status as well. This theology ultimately led to the indulgence system to which Martin Luther and other Reformers strongly objected. The Catholic Church taught that it had the authority to give indulgences—which remitted temporal punishment for sin, or in laymen's terms, time in purgatory—because through Christ it had the power to access that vast treasury of merit built up in heaven through individuals' acts of mercy and charity. The pope could dispense funds from this treasury to individuals, shortening their time in purgatory as a result. To give money to the church in return was considered a fitting act of gratitude—this was the theory.

In other words, for Reformation-era Christians, works of mercy were firmly and intrinsically tied to the doctrine of purgatory. Good works had the power to lessen time in purgatory not only because they imitated God and therefore made one more like God but also because those who benefited from such good works would then pray for their benefactor, and prayer was powerful. In return, those in purgatory were considered likely to pray for those who prayed for them.[31] It is not surprising, then, that in criticizing indulgences, Luther should have been led to reject the theology of works that made them intelligible.

MacCulloch notes that in the late medieval period, penitential sermons focusing on ways to achieve salvation were more common in northern Europe than in southern Europe, and the "purgatory industry" ultimately took more root there, which only made its abuses more visible. Did the proponents of the purgatory/indulgence system themselves unwittingly cast works of charity as mechanical tools to ward off eternal death and thereby help bring about a reconceptualization of charity as a technology that could someday be used to change society? This seems plausible, given that it was ultimately among Protestants that such a reconceptualization took particular hold in America.

In any case, the *sola fide* theology of the Reformers was the result of Luther's (and others') reflections on the abuses and corruption so evident in the Catholic Church. And *sola fide*—salvation by faith alone—meant that almsgiving no longer played a special role in putting the believer in contact with God. So the Reformers discouraged "mendicancy as the expression of a fundamental misunderstanding of justification; no human works, including begging or giving charity, could affect spiritual salvation."[32] In other words, the person engaged in an act of charity or work of mercy was no longer engaging in a "merit-worthy deed," for he or she could win no merit with God by his or her works.[33]

Protestant theologians also rejected the association of poverty with sanctity. So not only did Protestant governments prohibit begging, they began to require the poor to work in order that they should become as self-supporting as possible and acquire "a fixed habit of labor." While some Catholic governments at the time of the Reformation also began to prohibit begging, such policies did not tend to be very firm. "Begging remained, for many Catholics, a pious act that was deeply embedded in their religious tradition and practice."[34] Likewise, in Protestant churches the poor were no longer given a special place at funerals.

The consequences of these theological shifts took centuries to play out. It was far from the Reformers' intention, but the rejection of redemptive almsgiving had frayed one of the primary cords by which charity was tethered to traditional Christian theology. Ultimately, it would be cut loose entirely.

Chapter 2

Enemies of This Ordinance of God

American Charity from the Colonial Period to the Civil War

> Resistance to something was the law of New England nature;
> the boy looked out on the world with the instinct of resistance;
> for numberless generations his predecessors had viewed the
> world chiefly as a thing to be reformed, filled with evil forces to
> be abolished, and they saw no reason to suppose that they had
> wholly succeeded in the abolition; the duty was unchanged.
>
> —Henry Adams[1]

It is common for scholars to claim that colonial Americans' conception of charity was rooted in seventeenth-century English reformed Protestantism.[2] This claim can be misleading, for it is just as true to say that the American colonists inherited a view of charity rooted in the biblical tradition common to all Christians—and, to a large extent, Jews as well. As we saw in the last chapter, early Reformed thinkers and civic leaders recast traditional Christian teaching concerning charity in the nonsacramental terms that their *sola fide* convictions required, but they did not reject the entirety of the historic biblical tradition—far from it. At least until the benevolence revolution of the early 1800s, the theory and practice of American charity was recognizably traditional.

John Winthrop's famous sermon "A Model of Christian Charity"—written on board the *Arbella* in 1630 and the source of the "city upon a hill" metaphor so beloved by American speechmakers ever since—urges his fellow Massachusetts Bay Colony settlers to create a community founded on and overflowing with charity. As Robert Gross points out, Winthrop argued that charity and social hierarchy are intrinsically related. Because God has willed some to be rich and others poor, some to be masters and other servants, communities are characterized by an interdependence in which charity is necessary and fitting. Those who have been rewarded by God with material plenty are in justice obligated to help those who have not been so blessed.

There is little here that would not win assent from a fourth-century bishop or a twelfth-century nun. In the New England tradition as in the entire biblical tradition, charity was, as Gross writes, "as important to the giver as to the recipient; it was central to expressing one's humanity and religious faith."[3]

Colonial communities therefore saw themselves as obligated to assist those needy individuals and families in their midst—those persons who were *their own*. The institutions through which this assistance was offered varied according to political and ecclesial tradition. In Puritan New England, where church and state were thoroughly fused, the town itself took on this duty. In Episcopalian states such as New York or Virginia, parish vestries often provided direct, concrete aid (food, firewood, supplies) to those in need. Often, those who could not care for themselves (an elderly blind man, a disabled widow, an orphan) were taken in by other families, who in turn received compensation from the authorities.

This was the model for public charity. Private charity, aside from the church (itself often an officially public institution, of course), was seldom institutionalized in colonial America. Instead, it was embedded in mostly informal communal and familial practices, and it was made manifest in the care provided to the sick, destitute, and disabled. Motivated, then as now, by both religious conviction and self-interest, private charity centered on the family, which "served as a welfare institution, both for its own members and for others in the neighborhood," writes Amanda Porterfield. "Because the duties of motherhood were routinely shared, children called most of the adult women familiar to them 'mother.' Neighbors felt responsible for the sick and poor, not simply because compassion was a Christian virtue and not only because sufferings of one's neighbors were so present and unavoidable, but also because failure to take care of others produced ill will and resulted in lack of assistance when the donor, in turn, needed help."[4]

Whether public or private, as a matter of justice, charity was thought to be a local affair. Tramps and other strangers were not entitled to public assistance. If they had no visible means of support, they were often "warned out" of town or, if necessary, physically thrown out and told to seek assistance from their home jurisdictions. This attitude was not merely a manifestation of xenophobia, though it was surely partly that. It also reflected colonial Americans' fundamental unwillingness to disconnect the practice of charity from a localist ideal of justice—an ideal that answered difficult practical questions about just who owes what to whom. To indiscriminately care for another community's member would not only potentially stretch resources thin and deplete social capital but also implicitly open this localist ideal to question.

In any case, American charity in the eighteenth century was almost always local.[5] Large gifts in the colonial era were typically given to "local institutions, in response to local needs," and there was significant social pressure on men of wealth to help provide for the community's most pressing requirements. As in ancient Rome, republicanism acted as a further spur to public beneficence.[6] But neither public nor private charity entertained notions of curing social problems. The limited goal of those providing charity was to alleviate suffering insofar as was possible within the constraints of social order—constraints provided largely by particular localist and Protestant assumptions.

One area in which the colonists' Protestantism made an especially distinctive difference was in their attitudes toward begging. Unlike Catholics, who still subscribed to the reviled doctrine of redemptive almsgiving, the Puritans thought it monstrous not to discriminate between the worthy and the unworthy poor. This distinction had been enshrined in the English Poor Law, which the Puritans had adapted to their own circumstances. Wandering beggars were *especially* unworthy, since they had "broken the bonds of community and rejected the idea of diligently working in a calling."[7] "Throughout the Middle Ages," notes Kenneth Kusmer, "social custom and Catholic theology promoted a lenient attitude toward begging, and during the thirteenth and fourteenth centuries the mendicant orders even raised begging to the level of a spiritual principle, as one way of imitating Christ. In many ways,

Protestantism was very far from being a complete break with the medieval worldview, but its new emphasis on the efficacious spiritual value of work set it apart from Catholic views." Thus, for example, the English Calvinist William Perkins referred to beggars and tramps as "enemies of this ordinance of God."[8]

It is worth noting that in practice, many colonial citizens, including Protestants, gave food and money to beggars and other representatives of the "unworthy" poor anyway, and various ministers and authorities counseled that everyone deserved relief—even those whose problems stemmed from vice.[9] Especially in coastal towns, a good deal of vagrancy and begging was more or less permitted because of the "general belief that poverty and crime could never be completely expunged from the social order and sometimes even served a religious purpose." Kusmer maintains that "[i]n the late eighteenth century, the stern language of the vagrancy codes was mitigated by class solidarity and traditional practices of charitable giving."[10] Likewise, distinctions between the worthy and unworthy poor were not often made when private parties or committees of citizens distributed food and goods to the needy. The result was a colonial populace that was less hostile and more charitable toward beggars, the poor, and the homeless than official attitudes and laws might lead one to believe.[11] By and large, such groups would encounter greater hostility and suspicion in the nineteenth century than in the eighteenth century, as traditional notions of charity were eroded.

It was not until the middle of the eighteenth century, as capitalism became more sophisticated and Enlightenment ideas more pervasive, that voluntary private associations—the entities that today we regard as the heart of civil society—began to mushroom in American life. Modeled on the joint-stock companies that pooled capital in order to achieve what an individual's capital could not, many of these associations tended to aim at larger, more ambitious goals than did churches, local authorities, or the relatively few private charitable institutions then extant. These new associations sought to advance social well-being or the public good more generally rather than simply to alleviate individual suffering. The organizers of London's Foundling Hospital (1739), for example, believed that educating and nurturing abandoned children would not only ease their plights but also pay off in a more educated and able workforce.

One of the earliest similar American institutions was the Society for Encouraging Industry and Employing the Poor, formed by Boston merchants in 1756. As its name suggests, its purpose was not to provide relief to the poor but to help them "become useful and valuable members of the community" by putting them to work in linen mills. The prevailing mood of this new society is indicated by the title of a sermon delivered to its members by Charles Chauncey in 1752: "The Idle Poor secluded from the Bread of Charity by the Christian Law." In other words, it was in keeping with official Puritan attitudes toward the poor.

Benjamin Franklin—the "patron saint of American philanthropy," in Daniel Boorstin's words—offers a splendid example of the new way of thinking that took root during the Revolutionary period and illustrates well its debt to the Enlightenment. Franklin's goal was to improve the human condition by encouraging the growth of those institutions and practices that contributed to greater comfort and health. Franklin established the first volunteer fire company and the first subscription library in America. He founded the institution that became the University of Pennsylvania as a free school for poor children. And he very much believed in trying to eliminate poverty by helping the poor help themselves—not by providing them with direct aid. Much like his later admirer Andrew Carnegie, "to Franklin, traditional charity—alms—was self-defeating; the money would be here today and gone tomorrow, and the poor would be as dependent as ever. By contrast, philanthropy removed the conditions it addressed; in its successful wake, charity would go out of business."[12] Here as elsewhere, Franklin presented himself as an innovator at odds with traditional practice. "I am for doing good to the poor," he wrote, "but I differ in opinion of the means. I think the best way of doing good to the poor, is not making them easy *in* poverty, but leading or driving them *out* of it. In my youth I traveled much, and I observed in different countries, that the more public provisions were made for the poor, the less they provided for themselves, and of course became poorer. And, on the contrary, the less was done for them, the more they did for themselves, and became richer."[13]

It is no surprise that such a committed and energetic man of the Enlightenment as Franklin should have come to see charity through a consequentialist lens. Thanks to Enlightenment optimism that the human condition could be radically improved, the social consequences of charitable practices inevitably gained new importance. With the marginalization of theological considerations, it was increasingly possible to imagine using technological rationality in the service of the public good. The unleashing of that imagination depended on discrediting—or at least achieving further distance from—the traditional theological framework for charity.

But in bringing about that distance, it was not just the technological rationality celebrated by the Enlightenment and the models provided by the economic institutions of industrial capitalism that played a significant role. Christian leaders themselves collaborated in this process. In fact, the Second Great Awakening arguably played as large a role as did capitalism and Enlightenment secularism in transforming how Americans thought about voluntary giving.

Beginning in the very late 1700s and peaking in the 1820s and 1830s, the religious movement now known as the Second Great Awakening was led by revivalists such as Charles Grandison Finney. Preachers like Finney taught that Christians ought to be committed "to the universal reformation of the world."[14] Their duty was to remake society (Mary Lyon, founder of Mount Holyoke Female Seminary, told her donors that they were "advancing as fast as possible, the renovation of the whole human family"), a job seemingly bigger than what could be performed through the practices and institutions of charity as historically conceived and practiced.[15] In response, as Alexis de Tocqueville famously noted with much approbation, Americans organized. "Americans of all ages, all conditions, and all dispositions constantly form associations," Tocqueville observed in *Democracy in America*.[16] He does not seem to have realized how relatively new this habit was nor how much it owed to the religious awakening washing over American society.

Many early nineteenth-century American associations had strictly bounded and local ends—"to give entertainments, to found seminaries, to build inns, to construct churches," in Tocqueville's words. But many others— especially newer types only recently arisen—were more ambitious. Inspired by the nation's waxing evangelical fervor, "during the decades before the Civil War, Americans organized crusades to end poverty and drunkenness, enforce the Sunday Sabbath, abolish slavery, emancipate women, rehabilitate criminals, cure insanity, and ensure world peace." Nearly all antebellum reformers, in fact, "believed that it was possible not only to change the world, but also to perfect it,"[17] and they spoke of their work interchangeably as "benevolent" or "philanthropic" rather than simply charitable.[18] In other words, modern philanthropy's focus on getting at "root causes" owes much not only to the Enlightenment tradition represented by Franklin but also to the evangelical movement represented by Finney, Lyman and Henry Ward Beecher, Timothy Dwight, and other prominent figures associated with the Second Great Awakening.

Millennialism was one of the core beliefs embraced by these leaders. It posited that there would be a thousand-year reign of righteousness, justice, and peace before Christ's Final Judgment. Even philanthropists whose Christian belief was lukewarm or nonexistent embraced a variety of this millennialism in believing in the inevitability of the advent of a better world. Millennialism was easily assimilable to the broader ideology of progress to which many nineteenth-century Americans subscribed.

Millennialism was not a new doctrine, but it gained special psychic force and plausibility in the United States through its association with Americans' strong belief in their exceptionalism—and in the divine source of this exceptionalism. Furthermore, "millennialism provided a justification for action. Antebellum adherents believed that people should work to realize their vision of a perfect society rather than passively waiting for the millennium to arrive."[19] Older notions, like John Winthrop's, that social hierarchies and roles were more or less fixed or that poverty and suffering were intrinsically part of this world's fallen order were rejected by millennialists, for whom a rejection of Calvinist predestination meant also a zealous embrace of the doctrine of free will. Individuals—including the poor, the idle, and the vicious—could *change*. The suffering could *do* something about their plight. They could learn good habits, improve their self-discipline, and sober up. It was the Christian reformer's job to help.[20]

Thanks to all these forces—the new organizational models provided by industrial capitalism, the new optimism for social improvement characteristic of Enlightenment thought, the belief in social perfection advanced by evangelical millennialism—many of the new benevolent societies and charities that arose during the first half of the nineteenth century demanded a larger field for their activities than the local community. The stunningly vast scope of their vision demanded the development of new techniques that would make voluntary giving efficacious not just spiritually but materially—in other words, a more *scientific* charity.

By the 1820s, new, evangelically inspired associations with a national if not international scope of action had been formed, including the American Bible Society and the American Tract Society. For such associations, local charity was no longer adequate, especially when the foremost proponent of that outmoded vision of Christian duty—the Catholic Church—posed such a menace to American society.

As the historian John Pinheiro has argued, in the 1830s and especially 1840s, "anti-Catholicism emerged as integral to nineteenth-century American identity as a white, Anglo-Saxon, Protestant republic."[21] Voluntary associations played a primary role in promulgating that identity by providing "an important outlet for evangelical Protestants to voice their concerns while burying denominational differences." Sectarian rivalries could and had to be pushed to the margins when there were such important goals to advance as "evangelizing the unchurched on the frontier, saving the West from Catholicism, distributing Bibles and tracts, and preserving Anglo-Saxon Protestant culture. These were goals nearly all Protestants could support but ones which especially fired the evangelical imagination."[22]

In sum, these evangelical organizations not only typified the new spirit of philanthropy sparked by the Second Great Awakening's millennialism; they were also driven by a mission "to convince Americans that the Catholic Church was engaged in an unholy drive to topple the republic through deceptively benevolent institutions such as schools."[23] Anti-Catholic Protestants saw Catholic charity as a cynical tool by which the Roman Catholic Church sought to gain power over the people. This was a claim made, not in an unkind way, by William Prescott in his popular history of Mexico and less kindly by many others.[24] William Stapp, for example, "actually lamented Catholic benevolence because it had 'won for it the hearts of the unenlightened mass.'"[25]

Most evangelical voluntary societies of the 1830s and 1840s explicitly attacked the Catholic Church and its vision of charity, especially the pioneering American Bible Society and American Tract Society.[26] Many were controlled by nativists who tied their opposition to immigration to the need to reform Americans' charitable practices. They saw the acceptance of large-scale immigration as stemming from the same misconception as the practice of "indiscriminate charity"—as the result of being overly sympathetic to the poor at the expense of solving a more fundamental problem. Immigration was portrayed by nativists as part of a papal plot to fill America with "swarms of foreign convicts, idlers and paupers, the refuse of Europe" in order "to control our elections, fill up our poor houses, and harass our people and eat out their substance."[27]

Even nominally secular societies were often anti-Catholic. The Ladies' Society for the Promotion of Education at the West had as its mission the education of frontier Americans as a way of combating not just ignorance but "Romanism." Fearing that settlers in the West would only have Catholic schools as options, the society recruited Spanish-speaking Protestant white women to teach in New Mexico and Texas—America's newly "liberated" lands following the Mexican-American War. "Anti-Catholicism," concludes the historian Kevin Starr, "was an integral part of New England's mission to the West."[28]

It was also an integral part of the next generation's child-saving movement, which arose in the 1850s. The Protestant social reformers who led this movement appealed to the logic of the new philanthropy to advance the interrelated goals of suborning Catholic cultural reproduction and the logic of traditional charity. The child-savers believed that it was necessary to remove children from poor mothers so that a shiftless, dependent class of ignorant (which meant, in most cases, Catholic) poor was not reproduced. Led by the Association for Improving the Condition of the Poor (AICP), in New York City alone the child-savers successfully removed tens of thousands of children from their homes (sometimes, although not as often as they claimed, also from the streets) and sent them to good Protestant homes in the Midwest.

The AICP was representative of the new kind of "scientific" benevolent organization that arose in the mid-nineteenth century in reaction to the ostensible failings of "indiscriminate" almsgiving and "outdoor" relief, especially outdoor relief that did not discriminate between the worthy and the unworthy poor. Seeing poverty as the result of moral failing, the AICP provided relief to the poor only once they had been visited in their homes, deemed to be worthy, and instructed in the virtues that would lead them out of penury.

The AICP's representatives were often horrified by what they saw in the homes of poor immigrants—especially, it seems, those of Irish Catholics: overcrowding, filth, illiteracy, drunkenness. The list did not end there. The fact that the mothers in these families often worked outside the home was appalling, as were these families' superstitious religious ideas. The adults may have been beyond help, but for the sake of the children, something had to be done.

The American Female Guardian Society (AFGS) promoted one solution: it urged the authorities simply to take the children found in such situations away from their "dissipated and vicious parents." The parents involved were frequently not thrilled with this idea, and their resistance caused legal difficulties. The innovative leaders of the AFGS thereupon hit on another solution: in 1853 the society helped pass a new state truancy law in New York as a mechanism for initiating child removal. The far-reaching nature of this law was quite remarkable. It allowed any citizen and commanded any police officer to arrest a child on the street during school hours. The child was then taken to a private mission such as that run by the AFGS, and workers there had no obligation to contact parents. If the parents found their children, they could retain custody by promising to keep them in school. Those not found, or those arrested a second time, would be committed for the length of their minority to a Protestant institution such as the Home for the Friendless run by the AFGS or after 1854 to the Children's Aid Society run by Charles Loring Brace.[29]

The language used to justify AFGS's efforts to expand the placing out of children—that is, of taking them from their parents forcibly, often only because of poverty or truancy rather than abuse or neglect—is telling in its call for authorities and reformers to overcome their parochialism and embrace the new philanthropy. In its 1858 statewide convention resolution, AFGS "resolved" that "while the first duties of Christian wives and mothers lie within the home-circle, it should never be the boundary of their sympathies and efforts, but that they should seek as wide a field of Christian and philanthropic labor as their time and abilities will enable them to cultivate." The resolution goes on to say that removing children from bad homes is "the most *noble*, the most *hopeful*, and the most *satisfactory*" of "all the benevolent enterprises of the present age." Perhaps not coincidentally, 90 percent of placed-out children in 1856 were foreign born, according to AFGS's own statistics, and "a large majority Catholics."[30]

Was this entire effort driven by sectarian animus? Not at all, said the Protestant child-savers. To their minds, they were admirably nonsectarian in that they represented a number of different (Protestant) denominations, whereas the Catholics and Jews who criticized their policies *were* sectarian because they each represented just one sect! Furthermore, said the reformers, poor Catholic immigrant parents were in the thrall of priests, so their protests could be dismissed. "Charges of bigotry or anti-Catholicism were thus dismissed as yet another burden that child-savers must endure, if only to emulate the suffering Christ."[31]

In truth, the idea advanced by Charles Loring Brace's highly influential Children's Aid Society that most placed-out children were orphans was false. Very few were. Most of these "orphans" knew and lived with their parents—until they were saved by the new philanthropists. Maureen Fitzgerald maintains that "[w]hether the larger Protestant community understood or acknowledged it, reformers' efforts to dismantle poor families were central to their mission from the time the placing-out system began." The demonization of such families was central to this effort. Often, popular literature served as the vehicle for this demonization. "Every depiction of Irish women throughout this literature is constructed so as to invoke joy in the hope offered by severing the child's every link with mother, family, and community."[32]

Not surprisingly, the child-saving movement's commitment to a new kind of "philanthropic labor" ultimately provoked a strong Catholic reaction, in New York and elsewhere, that, in contrast to the child-savers' focus on "children's rights," emphasized parental rights, the sacredness of the family, and the proper limits of the state. Irish Catholic nuns themselves came mostly from poor and working-class backgrounds, and working in concert with Catholic-controlled political machines, they developed new institutions—orphanages, maternity hospitals, daycares—to care for the poor, regardless of their religion. Children placed into these institutions by their parents were not lost forever, as they were in the philanthropic reformers' placing-out practices; instead, they were returned to their families when their parents believed that they could provide for them.

The nuns' institutionalization system was profoundly out of step with the new benevolence. Progressives complained that the Catholic system did not means test nor seek to stigmatize those who used it, and therefore dependence on public charities grew (in New York and other cities, these Catholic institutions were supported in large part by public funds). Catholics were undermining the principles of scientific charity. But as Fitzgerald points out, the "nuns organized their work according to medieval notions about duty to the poor" and therefore had little interest in or attraction to the new philanthropy. "To deny charity was cruel and 'un-Christian,' not the hearty tonic Protestant reformers believed necessary to compel the poor to change their moral habits and behavior." Fitzgerald's characterization of the nuns' point of view as *medieval* is not quite right: the nuns worked according to a conception of charity that was older than Christianity itself. But in any case, the Catholic sisters were quite unconcerned about the growth of the public budget if it meant giving the poor the care they needed and deserved. As one popular Catholic motto put it, "Needs create rights."

The debate between those who favored purportedly scientific and institutional approaches to charity and those who wished to promote individual charity and personal encounters was not simply a Protestants versus Catholics argument. In the 1850s, that debate was still very much alive within Protestant circles as well. But as Peter Dobkin Hall writes, the Protestant partisans of anti-institutionalism never really organized effectively, perhaps because of the very nature of their position.[33] American Indians, too, were a special concern of many early to mid-nineteenth-century philanthropists. With many figures, especially Western newspaper editors, bluntly calling for their extermination, various individual benefactors and organizations advanced the notion that they be assimilated instead. Many Indian children were "saved" in much the same way that Catholic ones were—by being forcibly taken from their parents and placed not in Protestant Midwestern homes, which would have been a little much, but in Indian schools such as the famous one in Carlisle, Pennsylvania. Here again, in the words of Stephen Warren, "Philanthropists were both profoundly coercive and supremely self-confident."[34] They were certainly not inspired by the mythical modern spirit of liberty and scientific humility.

Prior to the end of the Revolutionary era, it was common and mostly uncontroversial for the homeless and other poor persons to be aided by private citizens. Often, the form of assistance consisted of food and fuel during the winter, especially during bad economic times. After the War of 1812, however, growing urban poverty contributed to changing views about this method of giving alms.

The New York Society for the Prevention of Pauperism (NYSPP), for example, was founded in 1817. Its mission was "not just the amelioration of the condition of the poor, but the prevention of pauperism itself." The society strongly criticized the "sentimental" approach to poverty that manifested itself in simple almsgiving and direct assistance. By the 1840s, other large, bureaucratic charities such as the aforementioned AICP had been formed and began to "dominate public debate over how best to deal with the increase in poverty and homelessness."[35] Thus, for example, the NYSPP tried to outlaw outdoor poor relief altogether, and the AICP would only aid the "worthy poor." The general scientific charity ideal was to place the poor in almshouses, where they could learn the "habits of industry and self-discipline" and thus become useful to society. Official, governmentally supported institutions were developed to care for the insane, illegitimate children, and unwed mothers. Professionals now oversaw the rehabilitation of these deviant figures rather than locals with little training or faith in rehabilitation.[36] Organizations such as these, supported by many among the wealthy and middle class, helped change American attitudes toward charity. "[T]he new philanthropic institutions reduced charity to a token act," writes Robert Gross. "Now, an individual could contribute funds to a house of industry for the poor or to a refuge for unwed mothers, secure that he or she would never come into contact with any of the inmates."[37]

More traditional attitudes persisted, however. Especially in the South, where residents tended to have a more casual and less moralistic attitude toward the "idle poor," campaigns against idleness made comparatively little headway. Southerners tended to regard Northern humanitarianism as shockingly abstract and impersonal—an embodiment of the commercial, transactional values to which northerners were addicted. And the institution of slavery fit well within the older patron-client model of personal relations between unequals. "Visiting the poor, nursing the sick, caring for orphans; such activities remained at the heart of Southern benevolence" during the antebellum period.[38]

In the North, too, "a vast network of smaller associations, often at the neighborhood level and sometimes of an ad hoc nature," gave expression to an older model of charity that was less bureaucratic and professionalized. Kenneth Kusmer writes, "There were a great many New Yorkers who practiced what charity reformer Robert Hartley scornfully called 'impulsive' almsgiving. Such individuals rejected the new 'scientific' approach to poverty and were much less concerned than the more prominent reform groups with modifying the behavior of the poor to conform to a particular ideological agenda. The participants in these small associations believed that citizens should give to the poor out of a sense of civic or religious duty without questioning the motives or morality of the recipients."[39]

Opponents of the new, bureaucratized method of charity voiced concerns that this new model would mean that individuals would no longer be personally connected to or invested in the objects of their charity. Despite the growing strength of their opponents, in the decades prior to the Civil War they continued to form numerous grass-roots, neighborhood-based committees to give food, fuel, and clothing to the poor and unemployed—among whom were many who had been turned down for assistance by organizations such as the AICP, which rejected 75 percent of applications in 1858. Soup kitchens were a particularly common form of assistance.[40] Kusmer points out that "[t]he resiliency of these local philanthropies in the face of strong public criticism was only one example of the failure of proponents of the new 'scientific' charity to carry the day. Another was the strong backlash against attempts to eliminate public outdoor relief—the dispensing of money, food, or fuel by local government to poor people, often with little or no investigation of the 'worthiness' of recipients."[41]

Measures to ban such outdoor relief were often introduced by progressive reformers and then defeated by city councils. Reformers accused politicians of using such relief to buy votes—and they were to some degree right. Yet still this relief "would not have been so politically popular had not many favored a philosophy of benevolence that was distinctly at odds with that of the new charity theorists."[42] The urban political machines performed important work in helping to care for the poor. "One might even say," writes Walter McDougall, "that the otherwise crooked politicians performed better than federal and state agencies because they needed no paperwork, dispensed instant service, and treated their clients like human beings."[43]

As with Protestants and Catholics, the philosophical differences between the proponents of traditional charity and the new scientific charity manifested themselves starkly with respect to begging. By 1850, scientific-philanthropy proponents were urging people not to give beggars money or food. But other Americans disagreed. The *Cleveland Daily True Democrat* explicitly referenced Christian belief in counseling its readers: "Better to be a pauper in purse than a pauper in heart. . . . Better to be an outcast in society than an outcast of God. And we shall make ourselves one or both, whenever or wherever we shut our eyes against sinning or suffering humanity."[44]

In short, to its critics the new philanthropy was itself animated by the same spirit that animated the commercial society it intended to reform: the spirit of technology, concentration, and rationalism. For them, philanthropy's "achievements were purchased at an unacceptable price: the personal charity essential to any decent community."[45]

At the end of the Civil War, the millenarian lens through which the great conflict was commonly interpreted stood as an even stronger cultural ideal. The war could not have been for naught. It had to be justified, and the result was that Americans became even more confident in their role as "redemptive crusaders" at home and around the world.

Orestes Brownson had at one time been one of the brightest lights in the progressive reform movement. Universalist tracts convinced the young Brownson that Christians were not so much called to repentance as to reform. In the late 1820s, he was, in Walter McDougall's words, a "Universalist determined to reform the world by sundown."[46] But by 1849, a conversion to orthodoxy had led him to disown his former views. He warned his friend William Ellery Channing that "sentimental humanitarianism untamed by reason, love, and humility might easily degenerate into zeal, coercion, and violence."[47] "The universal lust to reform society, to reform other people in a spirit of ideology rather than faith, must at the last come to this," he concluded. "Love me as your brother, or I will cut your throat."[48]

In the 1850s Brownson elaborated on the differences between traditional Christian charity and humanitarian, reform-oriented philanthropy in the pages of his extraordinary periodical, *Brownson's Quarterly Review*. To Brownson, the advent of philanthropy in the eighteenth century was historically and philosophically aligned with a rejection of the supernatural. It "originated in infidelity . . . and attempted to do by human means what the Church was instituted by God to do. Philanthropy is a mere natural sentiment; charity, a supernatural virtue." Philanthropy rejected the idea of the Fall and preached human perfectibility. Under its tutelage, went the belief, natural reason would ultimately obviate the need for law. So "philanthropy went to work to reform—on a large scale; for philanthropy scorns small beginnings, and proposes always to commence operations on the masses."[49]

Robespierre was eighteenth-century philanthropy's most "ardent apostle," wrote Brownson. Understood as the motivating principle of the Terror, philanthropy had made the European continent "one vast slaughter-house; kings and nobles, bishops, priests, and nuns, old men and young women, were dragged to the scaffold, and the reign of love was drowned in torrents of innocent blood." Charity, by contrast, is both more realistic and humane than philanthropy. It "deals not with committees, attends not meetings, and is not to be seen on platforms, moving or seconding high-sounding 'resolutions,' but addresses herself to the heart of man; for charity is not puffed up, and seeks not to make a noise in the world." Charity intends to move others' hearts to God and thus to their neighbors. To Brownson, that was the only way in which real reform might proceed.[50]

In a later essay titled "Liberalism and Socialism," Brownson made an essential clarification. He argued that "philanthropy, when acting alone, seldom fails to make matters worse," but he had no sympathy for a theological conservatism that minimized the extent or evil of existing social injustices. "Let not the friends of religion and order have censures only for those who sought madly to remove" such injustices "by revolutions, and none for those whose vices and crimes caused them, lest they render religion and order odious to all men of human hearts." The urge to undertake philanthropy is a mark in favor of both liberalism and socialism, Brownson argued, but these ideologies err by trying to effect what can only occur through the supernatural virtue of charity.[51]

In any case, it was a "philanthropical" age, concluded Brownson, and the revolutionary philanthropic ideal emerged from the Civil War more confident and self-righteous than ever; the war thus magnified the threat to society posed by humanitarians. In *The American Republic* (1865), Brownson warned that "intolerance, intimidation, and coercion" could easily be justified as imperatives of philanthropic reform.[52] He feared that radical humanitarians would make war on the people in order to perfect mankind. Their vaunted altruism was the opposite of genuine love and charity—for it often veiled pride and the will to power. For this reason, Brownson concluded, Satan's "favorite guise in modern times is that of philanthropy."[53]

Whatever its cogency, Brownson's line of criticism—so characteristically intemperate and advanced in such a way as to alienate nearly everyone who did not already agree with him—found little traction among his peers. In postbellum America, scientific charity and the new philanthropy marched on to become a culturally dominant paradigm.

Chapter 3

Infinitely More than Almsgiving

American Charity from the Civil War to the Great Depression

> Fostering the good-for-nothing at the expense of the good is
> an extreme cruelty. It is a deliberate storing up of miseries for
> future generations. There is no greater curse to posterity than
> that of bequeathing them an increasing population of imbeciles
> and idlers and criminals. . . . It may be doubted whether the
> maudlin philanthropy which, looking only at direct mitigations,
> ignores indirect mischiefs, does not inflict more misery than the
> extremest selfishness inflicts.
>
> —Herbert Spencer[1]

The critique of humanitarian philanthropy voiced by
Orestes Brownson was not his alone. Brownson's views
were more or less those of a wide swathe of Catholics, Jews,
and nonprogressive Protestants in postbellum America—
which is to say, a sizeable minority. But their resistance
to the logic and practices of the new philanthropy was a
rearguard action, a countercurrent whose force, at least
within the most prestigious cultural and legal institutions,
was no match for the power of the main stream.

The new philanthropy had a special psychological
appeal in these decades. Following the Civil War, many

Americans sought to definitively purge from their society the corruption, abuses, injustices, and weaknesses that all too obviously continued to afflict the nation. After all, what else had the war been fought for if not to validate the idea that America had a special, "messianic destiny?" What else could the triumph of the saints mean than that the American nation was "bound to play a redemptive role in the sacred drama of world history"?[2] And how could its destiny be achieved if America did not continue to be purified? This was the Northern version of the war's meaning, at any rate, and eventually, after the passage of a generation or two, most Southerners also embraced it as their own. In historian Jackson Lears's analysis, the first few decades following the Civil War are best understood in terms of a mass emotional reaction to the war's devastation. In light of the bloody conflict, an idiom of regeneration and renewal had special resonance.

The new, scientific charity and, later, professional philanthropy clearly had unique roles to play in advancing this grand objective—not least in ensuring that everyone got on board with the new nationalist narrative. "The language of rebirth," writes Lears, "remained largely Protestant. Catholics and Jews might well view it with skepticism, correctly suspecting the assimilationist agenda that lay behind longings for national purification."[3] Blacks, Indians, Pacific islanders from Hawaii to the Philippines, and poor whites of all religious stripes had more reason for concern. During these years impeccably progressive philanthropists devoted to the messianic nationalist narrative would help fund "exterminist" projects, imperialist policies, and eugenic solutions aimed at bringing about the necessary revitalization of American culture. They would also devote huge sums toward the education of southern blacks, the eradication of diseases, and groundbreaking scientific research. It was all part of the new philanthropic package.

As we saw in the last chapter, even prior to the Civil War, the practices and theology associated with traditional charity had become objects of suspicion among America's more advanced thinkers. After the war, charity seemed not only counterproductive but also positively spineless. For postbellum progressives, social revitalization demanded a new kind of tough-mindedness, including the application of martial discipline in matters of philanthropy and social reform. A 1901 article by a prepresidential Theodore Roosevelt illustrates this way of thinking.

The truly effective social worker, wrote Roosevelt in "Reform through Social Work," must "possess common-sense sanity and a wholesome aversion alike to the merely sentimental and the merely spectacular." He or she must understand that "[t]he soup-kitchen style of philanthropy is worse than useless, for in philanthropy as everywhere else in life almost as much harm is done by soft-headedness as by hard-heartedness."[4] (One wonders whether it counts as hard-heartedness to wish for the extermination of nine of every ten Indians, as TR did.)[5] Soft-headedness was the great bugaboo of progressives like TR—a long list that would include, for example, highly influential figures such as William Graham Sumner, Mary Richmond, and Margaret Sanger. To them, the traditional practices of charity, and especially almsgiving, were antithetical to true reform in part because they were emasculating.[6] Charles Loring

Brace had said that "[t]he worst evil in the world is not poverty or hunger, but the want of manhood or character which alms-giving directly occasions,"[7] and in the late 1800s and early 1900s, there were battles within progressive circles whether the word *charity* was not too associated with feminine muddle-headedness to describe what they were engaged in at all. (The result of one such battle was the title of the journal *Charities and the Commons* being changed to *Survey* in 1909.)[8]

In New York, Roosevelt argued, traditional charitable practices were associated with Tammany Hall and the lower classes of people represented by (Democratic) machine politics; as such, they did not represent "benevolence of a healthy kind." Thoroughgoing "social and civic betterment" would therefore only be brought about by the leadership of the "independent classes of the community."[9] TR went on to profile several philanthropists doing the kind of work he thought commendable, including settlement house pioneer James Reynolds, whose work demanded "infinitely more than the sacrifice of almsgiving," since his settlement workers helped people not only to support themselves but to achieve "right thinking and right living." Roosevelt also praised Dr. W. S. Rainsford of St. George's Church for his embrace of the Social Gospel. "Brother can best help brother, not by almsgiving, but by joining with him in an intelligent and resolute effort for the uplifting of all."[10]

What looked like enlightened uplift to progressive reformers like TR, however, often looked like high-handed intrusiveness to those whose minds had been formed by a more traditional conception of charity—especially those on uplift's receiving end. George Ade

(1866–1944) was a Chicago-based journalist, humorist, and religious skeptic whose wide popularity rested on his ability to portray the interior world of the common man of the Midwest at the turn of the century.[11] Ade developed his own unique genre called "Fables in Slang," in which he used the argot of the Chicago streets to tell a story loosely structured along the lines of a fable but whose moral was often cynical, subversive, or ironic. Many of Ade's fables— once one gets used to the unique capitalization he deployed to make his irony abundantly clear—are still funny today, and the new Philanthropists (Ade would have capitalized the word) did not escape his notice.

"Once Upon a Time there was a Broad Girl who had nothing else to do and no Children to look after, so she thought she would be Benevolent," begins one Ade fable. The "Broad Girl" is one of the idle rich, a domineering dilettante and busybody. She is a fair if comical illustration of what the philanthropists of the time must have looked like to those whom they condescended to help. In Ade's story, she decides "that she would allow the Glory of her Presence to burst upon the Poor and the Uncultured. It would be a Big Help to the Poor and Uncultured to see what a Real Razmataz Lady was like." Finding a working-class woman in clear need of her assistance, the Broad Girl asks the woman if her husband drinks and what he does with his money. Receiving an unsatisfactory reply, she responds,

> "When the Unfortunate Man comes Home this Evening you tell him that a Kind and Beautiful Lady called and asked him please to stop Drinking, except a Glass of Claret at Dinner, and to be sure and read

Eight or Ten pages from the Encyclopaedia Britannica each night before retiring; also tell him to be sure and save his Money."

In this manner the Benevolent Lady carried forward the Good Work, and Dazzled the whole Region between O'Hara's Box Factory and the City Dump. It didn't Cost anything, and she derived much Joy from the Knowledge.[12]

Clearly, in turn-of-the-century America, one didn't need to be under the spell of Marx—or even a socialist—to view philanthropic uplift as an attempt to exercise class-based social control.

Ade, along with Mark Twain and others, specialized in puncturing turn-of-the-century philanthropists' pretensions by mocking their self-righteousness and pointing out the frequently self-serving nature of their projects. But a more important critique was mounted by those defenders of charity who argued that giving and asking for material assistance had to be understood first and foremost in the terms of a theological rather than political economy. The Episcopalian priest B. F. De Costa, for example, charged that the era's growing intolerance of begging betrayed "the growth of secularism and modern irreligion" and that "[t]he right to beg is as sacred as the right to life, liberty, and the pursuit of happiness."[13] And it certainly was not unusual for Catholic preachers at the turn of the century to counsel against a too-ready acceptance of the arguments leveled against traditional charity by reformers. Perhaps, wrote one in the *Catholic Homiletic*

Monthly and Catechist, "indiscriminate giving" really does lead to "social degradation," as the new breed of "economists insisted." But this was no justification for ignoring the concrete needs of the poor nor for failing to meeting those needs in a personal way. As was typical among Catholic priests, the pastor suggested that his listeners join the Society of St. Vincent de Paul as a way of maintaining the "spirit of charity" in a way that is "not simply philanthropic and humanitarian . . . but which is at the same time characteristically Christian," in that Vincentians bear charity and assistance through personal visits and engagement.[14]

Catholics, wrote another pastor, ought to be deeply skeptical of "the most sanguine theories of 'reformers' [who] seek to do away utterly with the 'problem of poverty.'" Utopianism wasn't the only concept that seemed to lurk behind reformers' ideas; they seemed also to view the poor as a mere "theoretical" problem. But the poor, wrote the pastor, "are with us, and their present wants clamor for our help. Shall we say that they are improvident, thriftless, intemperate? Then more loudly do their needs cry to us. We are not asked to encourage their vices, but to relieve their necessities."[15]

In numbers of Catholic homilies written and preached in the latter years of the 1800s and the first decades of the 1900s, the doctrine of redemptive almsgiving remained vibrant. Almsgiving and the corporal works of mercy continued to be seen as occupying a special place in the life of the faithful Christian. Little credence was given to the critique of charity leveled by the new philanthropists, for they seemed to miss the point: almsgiving and other works of mercy were profound duties, and those who fulfilled them in the "spirit of charity" would be rewarded by God.

Ecclesial writers did not ignore the arguments made by those who (like Steven Pinker today) argued that because science tries to get at the root of problems rather than simply relieving suffering downstream from their source, technological advancement does more to alleviate human suffering than do the personal ministrations of individuals no matter how saintly.[16] In 1887, this already aging argument was leveled by James Cotter Morison in a book titled *The Service of Man: An Essay towards the Religion of the Future*, and at least one contemporaneous reviewer was unimpressed by Morison's scientific imperialism: "The kindness and self-devotion which have been exercised upon those sick of the smallpox, before as well as since vaccination, are more important by far to man than the prevalence of the disease," wrote the reviewer. "It is a moral duty for those whom God has endowed with scientific faculties to use these faculties for their desired end. But to tell devoted nurses that for the diminishing of human suffering they ought to begin higher up and invent scientific methods for the cure of disease, is a proposal which only requires to be stated in order to reveal its absurdity."[17]

This was the view embodied in the Catholic charitable institutions that flowered in the years following the Civil War and, as we saw in the previous chapter, caused so much heartburn among Protestant reformers. Such Catholic institutions arose not only out of a blend of ecclesial pride and self-defense—their founders wanted to forestall the growth of anti-Catholic nativism and prove that their "child-saving" Protestant critics were wrong in saying that Catholicism was intrinsically antidemocratic, degrading, and poverty-generating—but also out of theological conviction: "Catholic providers believed caring for the poor was the true test of their own progress toward eternal salvation."[18]

The trustees of most Catholic charitable institutions in the 1800s were usually male members of the Society of St. Vincent de Paul. As Dorothy Brown and Elizabeth McKeown point out, like nearly all Catholics, the Vincentians' view of charity was shaped by their adherence to the doctrine of redemptive almsgiving. "Vincentians accepted the traditional Catholic understanding that the practice of charity was a form of meritorious service necessary to the salvation of their own souls. They believed that the 'help' of charity was always mutual. Persons who were better-off supplied material necessities and words of advice and encouragement to the poor. In return the poor were expected to pray for their benefactors, thereby helping to redeem the souls of the prosperous along with their own." Likewise, the Association of Catholic Charities of New York, started in 1902 and led by Teresa O'Donohue, explicitly engaged in charity out of a commitment to redemptive almsgiving and the associated belief that "works of mercy opened the church's treasury of grace." The Vatican granted indulgences to those who volunteered for the association, and O'Donohue argued that their availability had "been a great stimulus in the field of charity, as all members work with so much more zeal when they realize that all their deeds are bringing interest in the future Savings Bank of Charity and will be recorded on the last day."[19]

By the first decade of the twentieth century, statements such as these were pure provocations to the progressive reform community. The leaders of that community promoted exposés of Catholic welfare institutions that dramatically illustrated their deplorably inadequate conditions. On a theoretical level, they also criticized Catholic welfare institutions for their unscientific approach—that is, for failing to regard charity as principally a technology that could be used to either hinder or advance social progress. Catholic charities tended to accept "applicants without inquiring too deeply into their circumstances." They resisted means testing their clients. They refused to acknowledge that impoverished parents were ill-suited to raise their own children and should therefore be relieved of that duty by the state. And they resisted the professionalization and centralization of assistance that reformers insisted, not incorrectly, would lead to the more efficient delivery of services.[20]

The critics of old-fashioned charity found a financial champion in the Russell Sage Foundation, which put millions of dollars at the service of New York reformers' scientific charity organizations in the first decades of the twentieth century. Because these organizations had interlocking boards of directors, they were known as the "charities trust" by their opponents. Thanks to the Sage Foundation's support, scientific charity advocates ultimately broke the power of Catholic charitable institutions in New York when John Purroy Mitchel became mayor in 1914. The reformers' increasing prestige and power—combined with Catholic bishops' desire to gain more control over the institutions within their dioceses and the efforts of progressive leaders like Fr. John Ryan at the Catholic University of America—finally led to a Catholic embrace of scientific charity in 1910 with the founding of the National Conference of Catholic

Charities. Even so, by and large the practices of Catholic charitable work have, thanks to the substantial counterweight provided by Catholic theology, never become fully aligned with a purely technological conception of philanthropy.[21]

By the early 1900s, the Benevolent Ladies lampooned by writers like George Ade were still socially prominent, but "philanthropy" was coming to be identified with the social-reform work of the superrich and their new foundations, including the massively wealthy John D. Rockefeller. As Benjamin Soskis points out, Rockefeller "so vocally dismissed charity in favor of . . . 'scientific philanthropy' that some socialists, who themselves opposed charity as an impediment to radical reform, bestowed on him the title 'Comrade.'"[22] Not coincidentally, the Rockefeller Foundation, established in 1913, was the first to have as its mission not to support some specific community but "to promote the well-being of mankind throughout the world," a generality that provided the foundation with the broadest scope possible for science-based social innovation. Similarly, the Russell Sage Foundation was established by Margaret Olivia Slocum Sage in 1907 for "the improvement of social and living conditions in the United States," which it pursued in part by funding opposition to and lending a powerful voice against traditional charitable practices and institutions. And Henry Ford (Ford Foundation, 1936) lamented in *My Life and Work* (1922) that "[m]ore people can be moved to help a poor family than can be moved to give their minds toward the removal of poverty altogether."[23] He was entirely in sympathy with a technological, root-causes approach to social assistance.

For his part, Andrew Carnegie warned in "Wealth" (1889) that "[n]either the individual nor the race is improved by alms-giving. Those worthy of assistance, except in rare cases, seldom require assistance. The really valuable men of the race never do, except in cases of accident or sudden change. . . . He is the only true reformer who is as careful and as anxious not to aid the unworthy as he is to aid the worthy, and, perhaps, even more so, for in alms-giving more injury is probably done by rewarding vice than by relieving virtue."[24] Whether in the social or in the purely intellectual sphere, Carnegie believed that traditional religion stood in the way of progress. His Carnegie Endowment for the Advancement of Teaching (1905) played a key role in secularizing American colleges and universities by offering faculty pensions to those schools that removed from their charters any kind of denominational requirement or other theological test for faculty, students, or trustees. This was an offer that, under pressure from penurious faculty members, most schools found irresistible: today's Teacher Insurance and Annuity Association (TIAA) is the result.[25]

In their enthusiasm for finding permanent solutions to social problems, several of these prominent new foundations were soon attracted to the promising new science of eugenics. Far from being a distortion or betrayal of philanthropic logic, the eugenics movement—sponsored and funded by the Carnegie Institution, the Rockefeller Foundation, and individual philanthropists such as Mary Williamson Averell, wife of railroad magnate E. H. Harriman—exemplified where that logic could lead if not moderated by the sometimes countervailing logic of charity. Thanks largely to the assistance provided by these progressive and scientifically committed funders, an estimated 60,000 Americans were "coercively sterilized" in the twentieth century, "and the total is probably much higher."[26] Edwin Black is right, if melodramatic, in reminding the readers of his history of eugenics in America that "[e]ventually, out of sight of the world, in Buchenwald and Auschwitz, eugenic doctors like Josef Mengele would carry on the research begun just years earlier with American financial support, including grants from the Rockefeller Foundation and the Carnegie Institution."[27]

The advocates of eugenics were almost universally progressive critics of charity. Thomas Malthus castigated charity because it indirectly led to population growth and ultimately would lead to general misery. Herbert Spencer denounced charity because it allowed the "unfit" to survive and reproduce.[28] Darwin's nephew Francis Galton, a pioneer in genetics and statistics, wrote, "I do not, of course, propose to neglect the sick, the feeble, or the unfortunate. I would do all . . . for their comfort and happiness, but I would exact an equivalent for the charitable assistance they receive, namely, that by means of isolation, or some other drastic yet adequate measure, a stop should be put to the production of families of children likely to include degenerates."[29] Margaret Sanger declared that "organized charity" is "the symptom of a malignant social disease. Those vast, complex, interrelated organizations aiming to control and to diminish the spread of misery and destitution and all the menacing evils that spring out of this sinisterly fertile soil, are the surest sign that our civilization has bred, is breeding, and is perpetuating constantly increasing numbers of defectives, delinquents, and dependents. My criticism, therefore, is not directed at the 'failure' of philanthropy, but rather at its success."[30] Sanger realized that if philanthropy were to be a truly effective social technology, it would have to be more committed to applying the necessary means for the achievement of its ends.

Eugenics was by the early twentieth century a mainstream progressive obsession. George Bernard Shaw wrote in 1905 that "nothing but a eugenic religion can save our civilization."[31] Education activist John Franklin Bobbitt disdained charity because it countermanded the eugenic law of survival of the fittest: "Schools and charities supply crutches to the weak in mind and morals."[32] And these progressives were echoed and supported in their promotion of eugenics by many rabbis and ministers. The extraordinary success of the eugenics movement within the liberal Jewish and Protestant communities, especially, is an index to which the logic of charity was displaced by the techno-logic of philanthropy in the first decades of the twentieth century.

By the end of the 1800s, Christine Rosen observes, "the label 'unscientific' was becoming a term of opprobrium," and the cultural prestige of theology had become substantially diminished.[33] As a result of science's growing prestige and Christianity's declining social and intellectual influence, many of those Christian ministers whose doctrinal commitments were being reshaped by alleged advances in historical science tried to incorporate contemporary science as a whole into their theology and to apply it to the great problems facing a much more highly industrialized, more polyglot turn-of-the-century

America—problems that included lower birthrates, higher divorce rates, spreading disease, filthy urban slums, and a seemingly unassimilable immigrant class.

The social approach taken by the new scientific charity and philanthropy was therefore appealing. Just as certain religious dogmas had to be abandoned in the face of scientific advance, leading to a more reasonable and modern Christianity, so did traditional charity need to be reformulated in the face of what science had to say in the social realm. Thus reform-minded religious leaders actively helped lead the movement to replace charity with scientific philanthropy through organizations such as the National Conference of Charities and Correction (NCCC), "which in turn exposed them to hereditary explanations for human behavior."[34] In other words, as most of those involved in either movement could see, both conceptually and historically, eugenics and the new philanthropy went hand in hand: each involved overcoming the constraints posed by the personalist logic of traditional charity to bring about social transformation.

The Rev. A. O. Wright, for example, secretary of the Wisconsin State Board of Charities and later president of the NCCC, wished to quarantine the "defective classes" in "state-sponsored colonies." "Unless we are prepared for drastic measures of wholesale death or equally wholesale castration, we must cut off defective heredity by the more expensive but more humane method of wholesale imprisonment."[35] Francis Greenwood Peabody went so far as to argue that Jesus himself was, or would have been, "a scientific philanthropist."[36] And Reform rabbi Stephen Wise stated that he was not interested in "charity, but social service, building upon the rock of social justice." Eugenics was part of that "social service" for Wise and others, such as Rabbi Emil Hirsch; by the 1920s, Reform Jews played a conspicuous role in the eugenics movement. A number of rabbis were members of the American Eugenics Society, and others invited eugenicists to lecture at their synagogues.[37]

Because traditional charity remained central to its doctrine, the Catholic Church and its leaders were generally wary of the eugenics movement. Some, like Fr. John Ryan, did express support for certain goals of the eugenics movement (e.g., the elimination of disease and healthier families), if not its means. In general, though, Catholic writers and leaders adhered to church doctrine in their approach to eugenics-related issues, even before Piux XI more or less condemned the entire eugenics project in 1930 with *Casti Connubii* and despite new vistas for social reform opened up by Leo XIII's encyclical *Rerum Novarum* in 1891.[38]

In any case, concerns and fears about how heredity might be leading to racial decline and social ills were widespread among organizations dedicated to a more scientific philanthropy in the postbellum world. They give credence to Jackson Lears's interpretation of this period as characterized by a longing for purification. Charity workers were frequently confronted by criticisms that their work prevented natural selection from doing its necessary work in eliminating the unfit. Those persuaded by this line of critique—such as the National Conference of Charities and Correction—were naturally led to eugenic arguments so that they might prevent the spread of degeneracy. The Rev. S. J. Barrows said in 1888 that it was the NCCC's duty to "prevent" the nation's degenerate classes "from bequeathing this burden of imbecility to a future generation." Another early influential eugenics figure, the liberal Congregationalist minister Oscar Carleton McCulloch, argued that "charitable institutions . . . encouraged the feebleminded in their fecundity by providing unrestricted relief." Their unscientific assistance only made matters worse. McCulloch's solution was "to transform philanthropy into a discriminating, scientific enterprise." Practically, this meant ending outdoor relief; restraining private, "indiscriminate" giving; and gaining "hold of the children." His efforts led to the creation of a Board of State Charities in Indiana and ultimately to a children's guardian board for every county in the state, whose purposes were to take away children from parents deemed to be "vicious or incompetent."[39] McCulloch was no marginal figure; he became president of the NCCC in 1891.

Rosen notes that Christian social reformers realized that their focus on prevention and root causes was in tension with the "biblical injunction to succor the weak." Their answer was to recast individual charity as a virtue that aimed at "regeneration" and "redemption" rather than the alleviation of suffering alone. For example, Walter Taylor Sumner, a Chicago clergyman, made those who wished to get married in his church get a "marriage certificate" that showed their eugenic fitness. Like McCulloch, Sumner was entirely positioned within the mainstream of the new philanthropy; he worked with Hull House, for the United Charities, for the Juvenile Protective Association, and for various other new, scientific charities. His eugenics advocacy was part and parcel of a deliberate move to transcend the horizon of the local in favor of a nationalist vision. He urged his fellow pastors "to take up the questions and problems, not only of local needs, but of needs nationwide in their importance—questions which involved the integrity of the race, physical, social, and moral."[40] Charity's gaze was, in short, too provincial.

No foundation was more dedicated to using science to guide the new philanthropy than the Russell Sage Foundation, and in 1913 the foundation's director, John M. Glenn, gave a speech in which he "endorsed state-sponsored segregation of feebleminded men and women. 'Should not the churches arouse themselves and their States to the horrors of this evil and seek its prompt abolition by the Legislature?'" Many churches answered Glenn's question in the affirmative. By the middle of the 1910s, numerous religious leaders had all but dispensed with the theology that made charity central to Christian social action; they were ready to collaborate with eugenicists in a program of social reform. Canon Edward Lyttelton, an Anglican, even suggested that "the eugenics movement owed intellectual homage to Christianity for first articulating the idea that the human race could work to perfect itself."[41] Albert Wiggam replaced the Ten Commandments with a new set of eugenic Ten Commandments, which included "The Duty of Scientific Research," "The Duty of Measuring Men," "The Duty of Internationalism," and "The Duty of Preferential Reproduction."[42]

The American Eugenics Society sponsored eugenics sermon contests in 1926, 1928, and 1930. One contestant wrote, "Surely the Kingdom can never come in all its fullness among a people descended from the Jukes," the famous family whose alleged degeneracy was central to eugenics mythology.[43] Another wrote that the Good Samaritan today would not just care for the beaten man on the side of the road; he would also know "that his duty was to prevent those thieves from ever being born in the first place." Such quotes show just how far Protestant pastors had traveled from the traditional Christian view that the poor, disadvantaged, and marginalized were especially blessed. Instead, turning the Sermon on the Mount on its head, to progressive faith leaders they were cursed—obstacles to the advent of Christ's Kingdom. This was a view expressed time and time again by Christian eugenics enthusiasts, and while in keeping with the logic of the new philanthropy, it could hardly have been more alien from historic Christianity.

The eugenics movement was a spectacular, if hardly unrepresentative, example of how advocates of the new philanthropy were prepared to use scientific reason to ameliorate the new—or at least more highly visible—social ills ushered in by industrial modernity. But those whose thinking was more in line with traditional charity were not without their own means of confronting the unique social challenges of the late nineteenth and early twentieth centuries. For while the period between the Civil War and World War I is known as the progressive era for good reason, it was also the era of the fraternal society, a decidedly nonprogressive phenomenon that adapted old-fashioned charity to help meet the physical, emotional, and spiritual needs of millions of American men and women in an egalitarian, noncoercive way.

Fraternal societies were the most popular kind of voluntary association in early twentieth-century America, with the possible exception of churches. Fraternal life insurance societies had a combined membership of 1.3 million by 1890 and 8.5 million by 1910. In 1910, the combined membership of all American fraternal societies was thirteen million, and this number had grown to thirty-five million by 1930. One in three adult American males belonged to a fraternal society in 1920. In short, the fraternal-society movement was huge and inclusive, representing all economic classes and both whites and blacks. Insurance—both life and health—was the best-known service provided by mutual societies to their members, but other common services included orphanages, clinics and hospitals, and old-age homes.[44]

Fraternal societies were neither new nor peculiar to America. As we saw in chapter 1, mutual benefit societies were present in ancient Greece and had been common in various places and periods in the Western world at least since the medieval era. David Beito, the movement's foremost historian, argues that these societies grew explosively in America in the decades after 1890 in part because they "allowed Americans to provide social welfare services that could be had in no other way. The aid dispensed through governments and organized charities during the late nineteenth and early twentieth centuries was not only minimal but carried a great stigma. In contrast to the hierarchical methods of public and private charity, fraternal aid rested on an ethical principle of reciprocity. Donors and recipients often came from the same, or nearly the same, walks of life; today's recipient could be tomorrow's donor, and vice versa."[45]

In other words, American fraternal societies during the progressive era acted as institutions for the organization of charity, although that term was in bad odor by the time of such societies' meteoric rise; for fraternal orders the preferred term was *mutual aid*. Charity, to the vast majority of those who led and were members of America's fraternal societies, was conceived as a one-way street in which the recipient was not capable of returning anything to the giver. This conception is already therefore a nontraditional one, but since the basic features of the traditional economy of charity were no longer understood or believed by the time fraternal societies became popular in America, the term *charity* was rejected as denoting something too condescending and demeaning for respectable people to receive—and perhaps as something dangerous for a self-respecting person to offer. The assistance provided by and through fraternal societies was given in such a way that it preserved Americans' amour propre. Charity had to be recast as mutual aid in democratic, Protestant America.

Even under the name of mutual aid, the help offered by fraternal societies looked very much like traditional charity. Well into the 1800s, the societies' names reflected their roots in and connections to historic Christian teaching and practice: the Scots' Charitable Society, the Massachusetts Charitable Society, the Hartford Charitable Society, and so on. The earliest societies were also intensely localist—another marker of traditional charitable practice—and even as they came into prominence in the late 1800s, these societies focused on providing concrete material assistance to widows and orphans. One popular society, the United Order of True Reformers, described its ends as "unity, temperance, and charity," while another, the Ladies of the Maccabees, pledged to promote the three cardinal virtues of "Faith, Hope, and Charity."[46]

In fact, American fraternal societies seem to have only really started to disdain the term *charity* after it became associated with the new, scientific charity that came into prominence in the late 1800s. The societies' spokesmen during this period often criticized the paternalism practiced by the new philanthropists, even as they absorbed the stigmatization of poverty promoted by the same progressive reformers.

To understand this dynamic better, it is useful to refer to the distinction Beito makes between hierarchical relief and reciprocal relief. "Hierarchical relief," writes Beito, "was characterized by large, bureaucratic, and formalized institutions. The donors usually came from geographical, ethnic, and income backgrounds significantly different from those of the recipients." The new philanthropy was characterized by a hierarchical-relief approach. Reciprocal relief, on the other hand, "tended to be decentralized, spontaneous, and informal. The donors and recipients were likely to be from the same or nearly the same walks of life. Today's recipient could be tomorrow's donor. Leading examples of reciprocal relief included informal giving, church assistance at the congregational level, and donations from fraternal organizations."

Clearly, the practice of traditional charity has throughout Western history been more frequently characterized by a reciprocal-relief approach than otherwise, even when practiced by religious orders, in that these orders also themselves depended upon charity, and their members were most typically from the same social classes as those they served. Just as clearly, Americans generally preferred reciprocal to hierarchical relief whenever possible. Not only did members of ethnic communities hate to go outside their communities—and thus invite social disapprobation—by resorting to hierarchical-relief institutions, but the "indoor relief" typically provided by these institutions formed by the notions of scientific charity produced intense aversion. Not surprisingly, then, "[r]eciprocal relief was far more prevalent than either governmental or private hierarchical relief. Its most basic expression was informal giving, the countless and unrecorded acts of kindness from neighbors, fellow employees, relatives, and friends." We can never know the extent of this giving, but we know it was vast, and in Beito's judgment, the "self-help and informal neighborly arrangements created by the poor themselves dwarfed the efforts of formal social welfare agencies."[47]

Despite the fact that fraternal lodges gained much of their popularity from the unpopularity of moralistic, condescending hierarchical-relief institutions, they were certainly often moralistic themselves, often expressing their commitments to temperance, traditional sexual morality, patriotism, the rule of law, racial purity, and healthy recreation. Societies also acted much like agents of indoor charity in attempting to distinguish between the deserving and undeserving in terms of both membership and the payment of claims. The practices of lodges call into question the view of those who claim that the poor and working class were not interested in making such distinctions and that they were a tool of bourgeois social control.[48] But this does not mean that the left-wing critics of indoor relief and the social control practiced by hierarchical-relief institutions are entirely wrong, argues Beito, for

> [d]espite sharing the dichotomy between deserving and undeserving, the social welfare policies of fraternal societies, governmental relief agencies, and organized charities were not of a piece. Historians raise valid issues when they stress the patronizing and degrading aspects of charity and welfare casework during the late nineteenth and early twentieth centuries. This inspires the question of why exhortations by charity and welfare officials against the undeserving often strike such a false note to modern ears. Perhaps the answer lies not so much in the specific content of the requirements but because they came from outsiders, most of whom had never been poor. Charity and welfare workers could never truly comprehend the conditions of recipients or entirely win their trust. Understandably, the poor resented and distrusted the impersonal and bureaucratic system that distributed alms.[49]

America's fraternal societies continued to provide valuable and extensive social assistance as late as the Great Depression, when they by and large served their members well and when they served more orphans, sick people, and elderly than ever.[50] Yet despite the huge membership and clear achievements of these societies—their undeniable proof-of-model and extensive impact—they were apparently never seen as viable vehicles for philanthropic investment by America's grant-making foundations. It seems likely that they were unattractive partners because they did not aim to get at root causes.

This was the charge leveled against fraternal societies by a new generation of critics that had found its voice in the 1920s. By that time, such societies had entered the throes of a profound identity crisis, as reformers effectively criticized the efficacy of "mutual aid, family networks, and neighborhood cooperation as solutions to poverty and dependence." In essence, America's fraternal orders were faulted for failing to do something (provide "solutions" to social phenomena now thought of chiefly as "problems") that they had never set out to accomplish—indeed, that neither they nor their predecessors would have thought possible. Even in this nonprogressive world, the techno-logic of philanthropy had become pervasive.

Chapter 4

To Love and Be Loved

*The Growth of Professional Philanthropy
and the Case for Philanthrolocalism*

> What else do we all want, each one of us, except to love and be
> loved, in our families, in our work, in all our relationships? . . .
> Even the most ardent revolutionist, seeking to change the world,
> to overturn the tables of the money changers, is trying to make
> a world where it is easier for people to love, to stand in that
> relationship to each other.
>
> —Dorothy Day[1]

By the end of the Great Depression, traditional charity's
partisans were forced to become more creative in making their cases. Technology may have become Americans'
being, but the personal engagement, respect for human
dignity, and devotion to community associated with historic charity still had wide appeal. The case for charity
needed now, however, to be integrated with philanthropic
reasoning—or at least made in full consciousness of that
reasoning's power. It also had to grapple with the significant growth of the state.

Certainly, the one hundred years that have passed
since the beginning of World War I have constituted the

state-building phase of American history. Prior to the Great War, the United States mostly *were*; afterward, the nation *was*. World War II completed the creation of a unitary state presided over by a large and active federal government. Similarly, following the establishment and social acceptance of the first large, general-purpose philanthropic foundations, the early and middle decades of the twentieth century were a time of rationalization and remarkable institution building within the charitable sphere—the era in which the "philanthropic sector" as we know it today started to come into being.

The community foundation movement, for example, was born in Cleveland in 1914. It arose out of city leaders' frustration with (what they claimed to be) fraudulent charities, a lack of giving among the city's small donors, and duplicative efforts among the city's teeming mass of charities. As a solution, fifty-three charities were selected as worthy of Cleveland donors' support, and a coordinated fundraising appeal was made on their behalf. With the success of this approach, a new model for "community chests" and "federated giving" campaigns was born.

The leaders of these new community foundations tended to be heavily influenced by the cultural prestige of scientific expertise and organization and concomitantly critical of Americans' longstanding charitable habits and institutions. To these modern, businesslike, rational civic leaders, American charity seemed wasteful, corrupt, and appallingly disorganized. They admired the accomplishments of capitalist titans like Rockefeller and Carnegie yet were provincial enough to seek primarily to exercise leadership in their own communities—and to have residual sympathy for older traditions of mutuality and solidarity.

Community foundations had explicitly local horizons and ambitions, after all, and for this and other reasons (including the exit of many of the most talented youths from the Midwestern cities and towns where community foundations were most popular), from 1930 to 1960, they grew more slowly than did private foundations.[2]

As with the community foundation movement, the settlement house movement mixed the new philanthropic with older charitable traditions and practices. Jane Addams herself had divided sympathies. As a committed progressive, she was a key figure in the professionalization of social work and the growth of the welfare state. But of course, in line with the Hull House model, settlement house activists actually lived among and shared lives with those whom they sought to help, a model that put them squarely within the personalist tradition of religious orders and Jewish and Christian solidarism. Addams's own empathy for the poor and suspicion of the rich led her, for example, to criticize her fellow Chicagoan George Pullman's philanthropy as foundering on the problem that he was completely cut off from the lives of his employees. He tried to be "good to them" but not "with them," she noted.[3] She maintained, traditionally enough, that charity was not primarily concerned with the efficient provision of services. Rather, it aimed at "the creation of a community of feeling, a set of human bonds, which are in themselves perhaps more valuable than the services themselves."[4] In contrast to figures such as Theodore Roosevelt, she "resisted the martial ethic and sought less conventional models of heroism— models rooted in lived experience rather than the platitudes of millennial nationalism."[5]

The memoirs of Mary Kingsbury Simkhovitch further illustrate how the settlement house movement embodied tensions between the technological and the theological, the new ways and the old. Inspired by the example and ideas of Josephine Shaw Lowell, in 1902 Simkhovitch cofounded Greenwich House in New York City. Like Lowell, Addams, and other progressive reformers, she sought solutions to, rather than what she regarded as palliatives for, social problems. At the same time, she believed that intensely personal and local interaction offered the key to genuinely helping any community in need. "In the entire field of social welfare, it is daily contact that gives the factual measure of worth. And it is this nearness that must be preserved to keep the country from yielding to general ideas or notions at the expense of facts. Only as the public welfare is considered in small well-known areas will it be valid for larger units."[6]

For Simkhovitch, the question of scale was crucial. "Bigness is always suspect. The bigger, the worse, in general. For then one launches into the unknown. . . . One is not so likely to be taken in when dealing with people next door."[7] As an illustration, she discusses how one of her first projects was to launch an infant welfare clinic aimed at reducing the high infant death rate in the Greenwich House's neighborhood. This led to larger and larger projects until such clinics were implemented citywide. Yet despite her insistence that social workers must understand and respect local conditions, the point of settlement house work for Simkhovitch and others like her was to gain a better tactical foothold in displacing local mores and priorities, not to stand in nonjudgmental solidarity with a neighborhood's citizens. She sought to persuade the local community to accept and work toward reformers' goals and was not reluctant to use legal machinery to pursue reformers' ends.

For example, Simkhovitch recalled how she worked to expose and eliminate home-based manufacturing in the Greenwich House's neighborhood because it paid low wages and "was out of step with the major advances of American industry."[8] Her settlement house also reported illegal neighborhood stills to the government during Prohibition. And while she campaigned for the return of outdoor relief against the leading philanthropic voices of the early twentieth century, Simkhovitch had little sense of how scientific social work might be seen as invasive. (Consider the following: "Provision for the care of children of working mothers after school hours should be an all-the-year-round educational activity, developed especially with the end in view of increasing parental understanding and responsibility.")[9] Although she portrayed private, voluntary efforts to deal with unemployment as well meaning, helpful, and even "valiant," she also saw them as quite rightly giving way to government control and supervision. Virtually all new state and federal laws, agencies, and institutions were portrayed by Simkhovitch as advances.

The settlement house movement was, in short, paternalistic, but the negative aspects of this paternalism were moderated by its scale and community embeddedness. At their best, settlement house workers really did try to speak for the whole community. They sought to serve the common good and to promote human flourishing by putting themselves at the service of particular flesh-and-blood men and women. For Simkhovitch, who ultimately became an Anglo-Catholic, this was a way of uniting faith with works. Social work was meant to be a living expression of her religious commitments.

As voluntary associations and the philanthropies who funded them became ever more professionalized and strategic, Simkhovitch's contemporary, Dorothy Day, provided a more radical witness to an alternative vision of charity. With her mentor Peter Maurin, Day launched the Catholic Worker movement in 1933. At its peak prior to the advent of World War II, the Catholic Worker maintained dozens of houses of hospitality, farms, and newspaper operations. Reviled by many, including many Catholics, for their pacifism and anticapitalist politics, Day and her fellow Catholic Workers in fact witnessed the radicalism that always lay just below the surface of the Christian charitable tradition.

Day was raised in a non-churchgoing, intellectually serious household. Enrolling at the University of Illinois, she encountered writers such as Upton Sinclair, Jack London, and Prince Peter Kropotkin, and she consequently began to ask the same questions raised by Ben Franklin, Andrew Carnegie, and the many other critics of charity. "Why was so much done in remedying social evils instead of avoiding them in the first place? Where were the saints to try to change the social order, not just to minister to the slaves but to do away with slavery?"[10]

The saints that society needed, she decided, were present in the Socialist Party. Day ultimately moved to New York, where she wrote for socialist newspapers like *The Masses* and participated in various demonstrations and protests. She was a well-known activist and budding writer, but she was miserable. Soon after the birth of her daughter Tamar, her spiritual crisis brought her to the Catholic Church, where she would remain faithfully but not uncritically for the rest of her fifty-three years.

Day's conversion dampened neither her profound compassion for the poor and suffering nor her anger at their plight. She was highly critical of church leaders and members not just for neglecting the poor but for supporting the economic order that oppressed them. Inspired by Maurin, she came to see that the typical conception of Christian charity needed to be broadened to include not only the *corporal* works of mercy but also the *spiritual* works of mercy—including education, activism, and publishing. In this way, she was able to preserve the central tenets of the biblical charitable tradition while incorporating the concerns and insights of those who criticized this tradition as propping up an unjust socioeconomic order.

Day claimed that her synthesis was rooted in the lives of the saints and the social teaching of the church, especially as that teaching had been developed since Leo XIII's *Rerum Novarum*. Her goal was to bring about a Christian revolution, to build a new society within the shell of the old, by personally embracing voluntary poverty, striving for holiness, and serving the poor—and inspiring others to do likewise. "It is we ourselves that we have to think about, no one else," she wrote. "That is the way the saints worked. They paid attention to what they were doing, and if others were attracted to them by their enterprise, why, well and good. But they looked to themselves first of all."[11]

Day never came to think that the questions she had asked as an undergraduate were illegitimate; rather, she thought that the answers could only be found in the imitation of Christ. Day warned her fellow Catholic Workers that if they detached their work from their faith, they "become merely philanthropists, doling out palliatives."[12] Her "root causes" remedy was to seek holiness and to build up the mystical body of Christ. In practice, this meant starting houses of hospitality, an idea inspired both by Maurin and by Rose Hawthorne, Nathaniel's daughter, who as a nun had established a hospice for the poor suffering from cancer. The *Catholic Worker* newspaper also encouraged parishes to start maternity guilds for poor mothers. Farms were started as experiments in the achievement of economic self-sufficiency. And always there were retreats, newspapers, lectures, protests, and picket lines.

Day's radicalism was uncompromising. The so-called counsels of perfection—embodied in Christ's call to the rich young man to "give all that you have to the poor, and follow me"—were obligatory for everyone, not just a few, she fervently believed. Far from thinking of charitable acts and voluntary giving as offering a way to lift all out of poverty, she saw such acts and giving as a way for the giver to enter *into* poverty, to share it with the suffering, to bring more love into the world. "When we succeed in persuading our readers to take the homeless into their homes," she wrote, "then we will be known as Christians because of the way we love one another. We should have hospices in all the poor parishes. We should have coffee lines to take care of the transients; we should have this help we give sweetened by mutual forbearance and Christian Charity."[13]

No other twentieth-century American so thoroughly challenged while simultaneously deepening the tenets of both traditional charity and scientific philanthropy. But Day's was not a vision that appealed to existing institutions working within either tradition—especially the latter. No matter what Day or any other critic had to say, in the early, middle, and later decades of the twentieth century, philanthropic foundations grew at a startling pace in both size and number. Successfully warding off various populist assaults and ultimately securing highly favorable tax treatment under federal law, the number of foundations grew from 25,000 in 1968 to 86,000 in 2012.[14] The success with which these foundations have met in achieving philanthropy's distinctive goal of solving social problems is open to question and is therefore often debated. But there is no doubt that today, America's leading foundations are highly sophisticated and constitute a distinctive sector of the economy. They are thoroughly professionalized and betray an increasing fluency in evaluative metrics and other trappings of corporate culture. They also characteristically see themselves as partners with the state—as loci of social experimentation that the state can bring to scale. As such, they have the same need as the state to "see" the social landscape that they wish to manipulate and control.[15]

This observation brings us to a final aspect of philanthropic logic that has not yet been a subject of wide discussion: its severe epistemic limitations. Since the middle of the twentieth century, thinkers from Michael Oakeshott to Michael Polanyi to Wendell Berry have examined the limits of the model of knowledge presupposed and advanced by modern scientific reason, especially as that model is applied to society and human persons. Their critiques raise especially important questions about the suitability and adequacy of the philanthropic approach.

The sociologist James C. Scott's critique of what he calls the ideology of high modernism is particularly illuminating in this respect. High modernism, Scott writes,

> is best conceived as a strong (one might even say muscle-bound) version of the beliefs in scientific and technical progress that were associated with industrialization in Western Europe and in North America from roughly 1830 until World War I. At its center was a supreme self-confidence about continued linear progress, the development of scientific and technical knowledge, the expansion of production, the rational design of social order, the growing satisfaction of human needs, and, not least, an increasing control over nature (including human nature) commensurate with scientific understanding of natural laws. High modernism is thus a particularly sweeping vision of how the benefits of technical and scientific progress might be applied . . . in every field of human activity.[16]

Scott explains that a commitment to centralization lay at the core of high modernism—and that this commitment has been its greatest weakness. Rather than serving progress, he maintains, the centralization of authority and power has often only made things worse. The reason is that a vast sweep of human knowledge is practical and tacit rather than theoretical and explicit. The ancient Greek word for this kind of knowledge is *mētis.*

Thanks to the very nature of practical knowledge, Scott points out, mētis is inescapably local and particular. We always know much more than we can articulate in the abstract terms of scientific and technological rationality. "Formal order," therefore, "is always and to some considerable degree parasitic on informal processes, which the formal scheme does not recognize, without which it could not exist, and which it alone cannot create or maintain."[17] Unfortunately, "[m]odern research institutions, agricultural experiment stations, sellers of fertilizer and machinery, high-modernist city planners, Third World developers, and World Bank officials have, to a considerable degree, made their successful institutional way in the world by the systematic denigration of the practical knowledge that we have called mētis."[18]

Scott's work suggests that another advantage of charity over philanthropy is that the former leverages local knowledge and is more adaptable and context specific. Unlike philanthropy, charity is modest about the human ability to forecast and plan the future. And Scott's account of mētis shows why localism in voluntary giving has a unique and irreplaceable value and effectiveness. Practical knowledge cannot be "created and maintained except in the context of lifelong observation and a relatively stable, multigenerational community that routinely exchanges and preserves knowledge of this kind."[19]

The use of high-modernist ideology to justify radical interventions and innovations in the field of agriculture, for example, is illuminating not only because of its failures but because it has continually attracted philanthropic attention and investment. Lenin, one of Scott's quintessential high modernists, was nowhere more so than in his agricultural writings. His agricultural ideas were not notably successful in the unfortunate Soviet lands where they were put into practice, but they were shared by many progressive Americans, including great philanthropists such as J. P. Morgan, who helped raise $2 million for a 1918 industrial farm experiment in Montana and lost $1 million on the venture. Scott characterizes industrial farming as "a Soviet-American fetish," with Americans Mordecai Ezekial and Sherman Johnson even proposing to nationalize all farms in the United States under a "national farming corporation" in 1930.[20] To Ezekiel and Johnson, as with Lenin, the small farmer was a "drag on progress," and collectivization was demanded by both the course of history and economic rationality. Other American visionaries planned a 500,000-acre demonstration farm for Russia from a Chicago hotel room in 1928, not fearing, apparently, that total ignorance of the specific features of that piece of land formed an obstacle to success. The farm was a bust.

In fact, Scott claims that the high-modernist agriculture dominant from 1945 to 1975—the agricultural revolution largely funded and diligently promoted by American philanthropic institutions—has a massive record of failures. That skeptical view of the Green Revolution is becoming more widespread. Dan Barber (to cite just one example) argues that its consequences have included fragile monocultures, a huge loss of plant diversity, the widespread planting of crops that consume more water than will long be available, higher rates of diabetes and cancer, and a dangerous reliance on fossil fuels.[21] To the extent that these charges have merit, they may be seen as the consequences of the displacement of implicit, local knowledge by the more limited yet more technologically powerful, explicit, formal, and deductive knowledge promoted by the institutions of high modernism—philanthropic institutions very much included.

From eugenics to medicine to education to agriculture, over the last century philanthropic institutions have provided an important nonstate vehicle for the implementation of high-modernist ideology. The results have been mixed. As the economist Wilhelm Röpke pointed out in the middle of the twentieth century, it was "frequently in the name of abstract, general philanthropy" that "fanatical and intolerant mass hatred . . . such as national hatred, class hatred, and race hatred" was justified and excused.[22]

Aleksandr Solzhenitsyn also connected philanthropic logic to totalitarian practice. The narrator of his short story "Ego," set during the Russian Revolution, describes how the practical, small-scale social work of a man named Pavel Vasilyevich Ektov, "a natural-born activist in the rural cooperative movement," was derided by the Leninists then coming to power:

> [Pavel] never took up any of the grandiose, earth-shaking causes of the time. In order to keep true to his beliefs, he had to engage in some bitter debates on how best to remake the life around him and to resist the temptations and withstand the rebukes of the revolutionary democrats: devoting himself to social change by promoting only "small deeds" was trivial; he was not merely squandering his energy on useless work, he was betraying the whole of humanity for the sake of a

few people around him; it was cheap philanthropy that would lead to no great end. Now, they said, we have found the path to the universal salvation of humanity; now we have the actual key to achieving the ideal of happiness for all the people. And what can your petty notions of one person helping another and the simple easing of day-to-day tribulations achieve in comparison with that?

As the story moves forward, the peasants in Pavel's Tambov Province are systematically robbed, raped, murdered, and executed en masse by the communists.[23]

Today, a disdain for "trivial," "small deeds" is frequently the conventional wisdom within a professional philanthropy industry that prefers to work at the "systems level," to recall the Gates Foundation's reason for ignoring the homeless outside its doors while trying to end homelessness everywhere. The authors of the entirely representative *Do More than Give*, to take just one more example, call for a new kind of "catalytic philanthropy" that produces "systemwide change." They call for "proactive problem solvers" who "embrace a proactive, results-oriented, transformative mode of philanthropy."[24] This sort of language is representative of much contemporary philanthropic thinking. Where it is not utterly meaningless, it stands the risk of inspiring the kind of impersonal technocratic initiatives that can be horribly destructive.

The creative examples of twentieth-century figures like Addams, Simkhovitch, and Day; the insights of localist thinkers such as Scott; and the clear limitations, now witnessed over the course of more than a century, of a philanthropy uninformed from within by the logic of charity point to the need for a new model and justification for voluntary giving that creatively combines the best of the charitable and philanthropic traditions. Let us call this model philanthrolocalism.

Philanthrolocalism offers an alternative philosophical foundation and justification for individuals' and institutions' charitable practices. It posits that the primary purpose of philanthropy ought to be *to increase opportunities for and strengthen the possibilities of authentic human communion*. It happily draws upon the practical and technological advances of the philanthropic tradition, but it subordinates the technological metaphysics of that tradition to the personalist metaphysics, if not the explicit theology, of the Jewish and Christian charitable tradition. That is, it directs its gaze at particular humans embodied in particular places at particular times rather than at humanity, the nation, the global community, or any other agglomeration of humans in the abstract. It therefore has a strong bias toward localism. The philanthrolocalist concern is to promote human flourishing within the local community, not to "change the world" through the technologies of social entrepreneurship.

It is clear that whatever its other accomplishments, the strengthening of human communion is not something for which our increasingly professionalized philanthropy can take credit. The philanthropy sector has almost tripled in size, adjusted for inflation, since 1970—a period during which, as Robert Putnam and his *Bowling Alone* coauthors are hardly alone in observing, American civic life has suffered terrible erosion. The writers David and Amber Lapp, to cite just one example, have embedded themselves within a small Ohio town to report on the challenges faced there by working-class young adults. Their primary conclusion is that these men and women are suffering from isolation, from the absence of "supportive communities" and "the experience of solidarity, of being with others, of forging ties."[25] A philanthropic community that has opposed itself to the spiritual wisdom embodied in the logic and ends of charity has difficulty understanding, much less helping to alleviate, this kind of situation.

Contemporary philanthropy's roots lie in a philosophical tradition that holds that everyone ought to be able to look out for himself or herself; those who cannot must be educated if possible and institutionalized (or eliminated) if necessary. This worldview is one of the conceptual fruits of possessive individualism. But the first and most basic principle of philanthrolocalism is the insight that we are not our own. Affirmed in the twentieth century most cogently, perhaps, by the Canadian philosopher George Parkin Grant, this insight finds perennial expression in our philosophical heritage and in every one of the world's great religious and wisdom traditions. It means that every one of us owes, in part, our achievements, successes, prosperity, and even our very being to others. Most of us intuit this, which is why our natural response to success includes an expression of gratitude to those who helped make it possible.

There is no such thing (despite the insistence of countless business biographies) as a "self-made man." We are the products of others: of the ancestors and families who gave us life and raised us, of the neighborhoods and communities and towns and cities that helped form us, of the agricultural and ecological contexts that have sustained us, of the schools and teachers that have educated us, of the artists and musicians who have provided us with transcendent insights, of the religious institutions that have taught us about self-limitation and the divine.

The philanthrolocalist acknowledges the fact that we do not make ourselves. Most people, in fact, naturally wish to "give back" to the people and places that helped form them. Philanthrolocalism affirms and encourages this completely natural and human desire—rather than belittling it or sneering at it, as the culture of contemporary philanthropy too often does. Financially supporting our own places is one way in which we can acknowledge and express our gratitude to that which has made us what and who we are—and to that which continues to sustain us.

A second philanthrolocalist principle—one that stands in direct contrast to the impersonal, utilitarian ethic of effective altruism—is that we have a primary responsibility to look after that which is closest to us. Certain obligations and duties are not chosen but are nevertheless ours by reason of birth and propinquity. That may not be fair, but it is still something that we all instinctively understand, even when we rebel against it.

These two principles are important, because contemporary philanthropists often tend to think of themselves as having no real obligations at all. They fret about having no real guide for their giving. Recognizing this purported conundrum, authors Thomas Tierney and Joel Fleishman, in their book *Give Smart*, call on philanthropists to be accountable to self-imposed "excellence"—not, one notes, to the moral obligations that are theirs simply by virtue of to whom and where they belong.[26]

A third principle consists in a recognition that the forces of modern life have conspired to fragment and weaken many, if not most, local communities. Industrialization, globalization, mass culture, modern warfare, and geographic mobility, to name a few factors, have enriched the lives of a few fortunate places while depleting the vitality of many, many others. Giving locally is one way in which we can help rebuild communities across America, counteracting many of the trends that have weakened American democracy and created a very real kind of social injustice.

The prioritization of local giving may be denigrated by the philanthropy industry because of a prejudice against rootedness. Philanthropy executives are often suspicious of local communities. They tend to view such communities as bastions of racism, sexism, fundamentalism, and generally dangerous narrow-mindedness. The philanthropist's role becomes that of weakening these communities, thereby making it possible to bring enlightenment to their members. For example, Tachi Yamada, president of the Gates Foundation's Global Health Initiative, was asked by the *New York Times* in 2010 what he looked for in new hires. His answer was revealing:

> I've made an observation about people. There are people who have moved. Take somebody who's a child of an Army officer—they will have moved 10 times in their lives. And then there are people who've been born and raised and educated and employed in one town their whole lives. Who do you think is willing to change? I think, in this modern world, you really have to be sure that your work force has the experience of being elsewhere. That experience then has the ability to ensure that you will be comfortable with change.[27]

There are, however, as James C. Scott, Wendell Berry, and many other contemporary thinkers are beginning to rediscover, certain unique advantages to be gained by long habitation in a particular place, not the least of which are complex knowledge and affection. Why would you care deeply about a place you intend to leave at the next good opportunity? But to philanthropic executives like Yamada attached to a narrow view of the human condition, the human attachments that come with such a life are only stifling, never liberating.

This suspicion of real, concrete local communities is one reason today's Big Philanthropy stands opposed to philanthrolocalism. Another is that when they focus on local giving, individual donors and charitable foundations tend not to need much guidance from philanthropic experts. It's easier to spot local needs, to evaluate which local organizations are most effective, and to assess the impact of one's local giving (especially if you've been living in one place for a while) than it is to do any of these things with respect to national and international groups. Sophisticated metrics showing impact become luxuries, not necessities. The questions that are asked when one is giving locally also tend to be less abstract—and therefore more readily answerable on the basis of everyday logic and common sense.

To practice philanthrolocalism requires no special training or adherence to some secret teaching. When you give locally, or when you engage personally and lovingly with others needing help, you are practicing philanthrolocalism. The primary obstacle to practicing philanthrolocalism, in fact, may be a sense that what you are doing is not "important" or "strategic" enough—that local giving is for rubes. To be a philanthrolocalist, you must educate yourself *out* of the antilocalist prejudices that pervade American education and culture and relearn the natural human language and sentiments of place.

How do you do that? The progressive philanthropy scholar Pablo Eisenberg gave wise advice to Owen Lopez when Lopez became the executive director of the McCune Charitable Foundation: "You identify people in community doing what needs to be done; you give them money; and you shut up."[28]

The effective donor need not—and probably should not—want to "change the world." It's hard enough to improve one's own block. Presidents and kings typically fail to "change the world," at least in a positive way, despite the best of intentions. The world—the social world, the world of human behavior, or what we call *culture*—is infinitely complex and infinitely beyond the comprehension of any one person or group of persons. As sociologist James Davison Hunter has shown, it is therefore inherently refractory to being shaped intentionally and decisively by anyone.[29] And as all localists know, the bigger you think, the more likely you are to fail—or to bring about unforeseen consequences, some of which may be negative. It does not reflect poorly on the local thinker's cognitive powers to restrict his or her giving to local matters; rather, it reflects his or her humility and wisdom.

There are many specific examples of donors acting consciously, intelligently, and creatively to strengthen their own places. For example, David Van Andel has said that his parents, Jay and Betty, "founded the Van Andel

Institute in Grand Rapids not because it was the easiest place to establish an unknown biomedical research institute, but because they wanted to share it with the community that had sustained and nurtured them." (It is a measure of the need today for a self-conscious philanthrolocalism that, as the *Grand Rapids Press* reports, the rising generation of West Michigan philanthropists "tend to be more attracted to global rather than local issues."[30])

As recent books like *Hollowing Out the Middle* have made abundantly clear,[31] America's rural areas, small towns, and midsized cities located away from today's "superstar cities" and "means metros" (to use Richard Florida's terminology) are losing their smartest, most talented, most ambitious young people.[32] And they have been for some time. This is the downside of the highly mobile, extraordinarily meritocratic society that America has become. Theorists like Florida celebrate the new segregation of the smart and upwardly mobile from mere commoners, but thinkers like Christopher Lasch and Bill Kauffman have argued cogently that this is not a trend that augurs well for democracy or community.[33]

Some donors have started to do something about it. In the economically depressed area of Tamaqua, Pennsylvania, two local foundations have provided extremely generous scholarships for local students to attend local colleges and universities. The result has been that dramatically fewer kids have decided to pick up roots, never to return, and the scholarship opportunities have even led to some families relocating to the area for their children's high school years.[34]

Needless to say, these kinds of efforts could be taken much further. What if a local foundation decided to help pay off local students' college loans if they were to return to their hometown areas after graduation? Such a program would have to be designed with care, in order to avoid creating disincentives for colleges to give financial aid or to keep tuition low (in other words, if it were to have the same effect as the federal student-loan programs, then we're better off without it). But this could be an especially attractive option for the brightest of local kids who amass considerable debt attending liberal arts schools.

In any case, donors committed to helping a particular area flourish—that is, philanthrolocalists—need to start thinking about how to help keep talent, ambition, and energy at home. A wide dispersal of talent and intelligence is arguably as necessary as the Jeffersonian ideal of a wide distribution of property ownership to our national health. As Patrick Deneen writes of the Tamaqua initiative,

> Just these sorts of efforts could be the beginning of a virtuous circle, in which successful businessmen with a strong sense of place and gratitude for what they have inherited will encourage a similar ethic—including the encouragement to the creation of small, local businesses—thus fostering a similar ethic in a new generation. This was historically the responsibility of the trustees of communities—to bring up the next generation to become good citizens and trustees, some of whom would become the leaders and exemplars of their communities. At some point, they decided instead that the best thing they could do for their talented young people would be to encourage them to go away. . . . These philanthropists may be a catalyst to a fundamental rethinking about what should be valued.[35]

It is even imaginable that individual foundations and/ or professional associations of such foundations could voluntarily adopt benchmarks that provide standards for local giving—along the lines of the National Committee on Responsive Philanthropy's advocacy of governmentally mandated quotas for diversity giving. Besides being voluntary, and thus in line with the American tradition of free philanthropy, local-giving benchmarks would actually lead to increased *meaningful* diversity among grantees— including but not limited to racial and ethnic diversity.

As a response to the working-class social and familial breakdown they have witnessed in Ohio, the Lapps draw from the charitable tradition represented by St. Vincent de Paul and Dorothy Day to argue that what is most fundamentally needed is a "deeply personal encounter" between would-be helpers and sufferers. They suggest that young couples might intentionally live in areas where stable loving marriages are in short supply; that older married couples might befriend and offer informal mentorship to younger ones; and, more important for our purposes, that charitable foundations "could partner with a church or nonprofit to subsidize 'charity organizers,' who would live in working-class neighborhoods and perhaps even take working-class jobs. They would help couples in their communities share stories, identify problems, consult with peers, and decide on initiatives. They could also help to organize the worker associations that John Paul II described as essential, not only in negotiating contracts, but also as 'places' where workers can express themselves."[36]

The idea of a foundation partnering with community-embedded charity workers to provide assistance to those who need it is put into practice every Christmas by the Connelly Foundation, which has explicit faith commitments and is specifically devoted to helping those in the Philadelphia metro area. Tom Riley, the foundation's vice president for strategy, reports that thanks to decades of on-the-ground relationship building, "the people here at the foundation have developed deep relationships with the real charitable givers—the nuns, priests, ministers, teachers, and secular saints who work directly with the needy, unlike all of us check-writing dilettante foundation execs."[37]

How do you make the best use of these relationships? The tendency among today's most advanced foundations might be to help these givers set up impactful nonprofits with strategies to transform—or at least make a measurable difference within—the populations they work with. Or perhaps they would set up their own programs staffed by certified professionals committed to finding permanent solutions. They would at least require, as William Schambra points out, each grantee to invest considerable resources into the gathering of metrics showing their impact—that is, to "shoehorn its real-world work into the abstract, unfamiliar professional jargon to which data accumulators resort when they wish to generalize across . . . the varieties of particular experiences."[38] Most grassroots nonprofits, of course, are constitutively unable to meet this philanthropic imperative.

The Connelly Foundation is different. It certainly makes grants to those organizations it believes are effective, but it does not require most of the reporting rigmarole. Most encouragingly, it takes a disarmingly simple, charity-inspired approach over the holidays: it sets aside

$100,000 to be divided between twenty to twenty-five of the frontline workers it trusts, and it charges them with giving this money away in whatever way they see fit to those community members in need. The workers report back to the foundation about their acts of charity. During one recent Christmas, those acts included the following (names and some other identifying information have been changed):

- Mr. Thomas, who is homeless, received $50.
- Estrella Bernal received $200 for her child's dental work.
- Twenty of the students in a school will buy Christmas presents for special needs kids in the community.
- Hannah is a Nigerian mother of six. She works as a nurse's aide, and her husband is unemployed. She received $350 to help with her son's tuition.
- Deborah is a Haitian woman; she received $250 for rent. She is out of work and was about to be evicted.
- Nok is a Laotian woman; she received $350. She is the mother of two children who attend our Catholic school. She has another son, age three, who is mentally and physically handicapped.
- Li is a Chinese woman who last year witnessed the murder of her husband. Two men robbed the Chinese takeout where he worked. The couple lived above the restaurant with their three children, ages nine, twelve, and fourteen. They were arranged to attend a school free of tuition. She received $250 for her family's daily needs.
- A man who is about to be released from jail had nothing to return to—no job, no home, no family.

He received one month's rent on a room as he tries to reenter society.

- The Andrews family received $300. The grandmother is raising her granddaughter and needs the money to repair her stove, which was leaking gas.
- Torres family received $300. Mrs. Torres is struggling to raise her two daughters after their father was murdered.
- A mother who was robbed at gunpoint at an ATM machine received $500. She lost all the money she was going to use for tuition and Christmas presents.

This kind of direct charity would have been despised by the figures whose critiques of such giving gave birth to modern philanthropy. Yet despite a century and more of sustained effort and many billions of dollars, the Andrews family still needs a stove. Philanthrolocalist institutions like the Connelly Foundation, thankfully, are there to help.

To rebuild our communities and replenish our social capital, it is hard to believe that we need more of the technocratic ideas on offer from contemporary philanthropic institutions. Instead, we need more people to ask themselves just a few questions before giving from their resources or of themselves: Will this gift help to strengthen human communion? Does it witness to the *reality* of human communion—of the truth that we are not our own? Does it help me come into a closer personal encounter with others, or does it act only as a substitute for doing so? Will it contribute to the building of local community that is so necessary for human flourishing? Does it express gratitude to a community to whom I owe, in part, my being? And does it reflect the relative strength of the moral claims that others have on me? These are questions inspired by love—charity—rather than ideological ambitions to remake the world.

Notes

Introduction

1 Andrew Carnegie, "Wealth," *North American Review* 148, no. 391 (June 1889): 653–65.

2 This discussion of the Western Soup Society and its critics is taken from Kenneth L. Kusmer, *Down and Out, on the Road: The Homeless in American History* (New York: Oxford University Press, 2002), 29–30.

3 The statistics in this paragraph up to this point come from Foundation Center, *Key Facts on U.S. Foundations, 2014 Edition.* This document may be downloaded at http://foundationcenter.org/gain knowledge/research/keyfacts2014. Other groups, such as the National Center for Charitable Statistics, report slightly different numbers, but there is little material difference.

4 *Giving USA 2014*, Lilly Family School of Philanthropy, http://www.givingusareports.org/.

5 "Nonprofits Worth $887.3 Billion to U.S. Economy," *NonProfit Times*, October 28, 2014.

6 Arthur C. Brooks, "Are Americans Generous? Shattering the Myth of American Stinginess," *Philanthropy*, May/June 2006, http://www.philanthropyroundtable.org/topic/excellence_in_philanthropy/are_americans_generous.

7 Lester M. Salamon, S. Wojciech Sokowski, Megan A. Haddock, and Helen S. Tice, "The State of Global Civil Society and Volunteering: Latest Findings from the Implementation of the UN *Nonprofit Handbook*," Center for Civil Society Studies, Johns Hopkins University, http://ccss.jhu.edu/wp-content/uploads/downloads/2013/04/JHU_Global-Civil-Society-Volunteering_FINAL_3.2013.pdf.

8 See William Schambra, "The Coming Showdown between Philanthrolocalism and Effective Altruism," *Philanthropy Daily*, May 2, 2014.

9 Ibid.

10 The language here is tricky. I do not mean to suggest that by adopting a technological view of voluntary giving, philanthropy's advocates somehow successfully extricate themselves from adopting any theological claims. There is no neutral theological ground. I mean only to suggest that their theology almost always remains implicit, that it is typically denied, and that it privileges technological interventions to alleviate suffering or bring about social progress over forms of giving that privilege theological witness over this-worldly technological effectiveness.

11 Stephanie Strom, "Donors Weigh the Ideals of Meaningful Giving," *New York Times*, November 1, 2011, http://www.nytimes.com/2011/11/02/giving/donors-weigh-the-most-worthy-ways-to-give-to-charities.html?pagewanted=1&ref=philanthropy&_r=0.

12 "Interview with Howard Buffett," *Philanthropy*, Winter 2014, http://www.philanthropyroundtable.org/topic/excellence_in_philanthropy/interview_with_howard_buffett.

13 Olivier Zunz, *Philanthropy in America: A History* (Princeton, NJ: Princeton University Press, 2012). This book was supported by the W. K. Kellogg Foundation and the Charles Stewart Mott Foundation.

14 See, for example, Leslie Margolin, *Under the Cover of Kindness: The Invention of Social Work* (Charlottesville: University of Virginia Press, 1997).

15 The classic consensus-school text is generally held to be Robert H. Bremner, *American Philanthropy* (Chicago: University of Chicago Press, 1960).

16 I have in mind the work of thinkers like William T. Cavanaugh, Alasdair MacIntyre, David L. Schindler, Stanley Hauerwas, James

C. Scott, George Parkin Grant, Brad S. Gregory, Robert A. Nisbet, Wendell Berry, David Bentley Hart, and Patrick Deneen.

17 William T. Cavanaugh, *The Myth of Religious Violence: Secular Ideology and the Roots of Modern Conflict* (New York: Oxford University Press, 2009), 4, 9.

Chapter 1

1 Peter Brown, *Through the Eye of a Needle: Wealth, the Fall of Rome, and the Making of Christianity in the West, 350–550 AD* (Princeton, NJ: Princeton University Press, 2012), 54.

2 Andrew T. Crislip, *From Monastery to Hospital: Christian Monasticism and the Transformation of Health Care in Late Antiquity* (Ann Arbor: University of Michigan Press, 2005), 46.

3 See Brown, *Through the Eye of a Needle*, 68–71 for a discussion of how Roman citizens benefited much more from the generosity of the rich than did the noncitizen poor.

4 "[T]he concept of philanthropy in late antiquity was less an extension of any concern for the welfare of the destitute, than part of the desire to publicize one's social standing." Leyerle, "John Chrysostom on Almsgiving and the Use of Money," *Harvard Theological Review* 87, no. 1 (1994): 34.

5 Crislip, *From Monastery to Hospital*, 47.

6 St. John Chrysostom. Quoted in Leyerle, "John Chrysostom on Almsgiving," 32–33.

7 See Luke 17: 11–19.

8 Crislip, *From Monastery to Hospital*, 44.

9 Ibid., 19.

10 Ibid., 50.

11 Gary Anderson, *Charity: The Place of the Poor in the Biblical Tradition* (New Haven, CT: Yale University Press, 2013), 16.

12 Robert Louis Wilken, *The Christians as the Romans Saw Them* (New Haven, CT: Yale University Press, 1984), 14.

13 Ibid., 81.

14 Inscription CIL V.5262, in Pliny the Younger, *Letters and Panegyricus*, vol. II (Cambridge, MA: Harvard University Press, 1969), 551.

15 Wilken, *The Christians as the Romans Saw Them*, 47.

16 Anderson, *Charity*, 17.

17 Ibid., 49.

18 Ibid., 59.

19 Ibid., 25.

20 In the same letter, Julian notes that "no Jew ever has to beg." The letter was written ca. 362. See letter 22 in *Julian*, vol. 3 (Cambridge, MA: Harvard University Press, 1923).

21 Brown, *Through the Eye of a Needle*, 42.

22 Ibid., 41.

23 To disagree with this last claim, as some scholars may, means accusing most major figures of the early church of a rather astounding duplicity. Of course, early Christian leaders were well aware that their charity attracted converts, and bishops used charity to augment their authority and prestige, but this does not mean they would not have engaged in charity otherwise.

24 Anderson, *Charity*, 32.

25 Ibid., 69.

26 Pope Benedict XVI, *Deus Caritas Est*, encyclical letter issued on December 25, 2005, para. 23, http://www.vatican.va/holy_father/benedict_xvi/encyclicals/documents/hf_ben-xvi_enc_20051225_deus-caritas-est_en.html.

27 David Bentley Hart, *The Story of Christianity: A History of 2,000 Years of the Christian Faith* (London: Quercus, 2013), 205.

28 "Quite apart from the individual handout, an array of institutions, offering a variety of alms or assistance, had come into being well before the end of the fifteenth century. Wealthy individuals created pious foundations for the salvation of their souls, the prestige of their families, and the support of the poor. Craft guilds sponsored confraternities to promote public piety, to elevate corporate visibility, and to assist needy members. Monastic orders assisted the needy within their walls; some devoted themselves to the operation of hospitals and sanitaria. Churches and cathedrals set up tables, often in their own portals, from which food and money were distributed to those in need." Thomas Max Safley, ed., *The Reformation of Charity: The Secular and the Religious in Early Modern Poor Relief* (Boston: Brill Academic Publishers, 2003), 5.

29 Ibid., 14.

30 Ibid., 11.

31 See Diarmaid MacCulloch, *Reformation: Europe's House Divided, 1490–1700* (London: Allen Lane, 2003). See also the *Catechism of the Catholic Church* (Vatican City: Libreria Editrice Vaticana, 1994), 1478.

32 Safley, *The Reformation of Charity*, 7.

33 Cf. Anderson, *Charity*.

34 Safley, *The Reformation of Charity*, 8.

Chapter 2

1 Henry Adams, *The Education of Henry Adams: An Autobiography* (1918; repr., Boston: Houghton Mifflin, 2000), 7.

2 See, for example, Robert A. Gross, "Giving in America: From Charity to Philanthropy," in *Charity, Philanthropy, and Civility in American History*, ed. Lawrence J. Friedman and Mark D. McGarvie (New York: Cambridge University Press, 2002).

3 Gross, "Giving in America," 36.

4 Amanda Porterfield, "Protestant Missionaries: Pioneers of American Philanthropy," in Friedman and McGarvie, *Charity, Philanthropy, and Civility in American History*, 56.

5 Cf. Gross, "Giving in America."

6 Kathleen D. McCarthy, "The Gospel of Wealth: American Giving in Theory and Practice," in *Philanthropic Giving: Studies in Varieties and Goals*, ed. Richard Magat (New York: Oxford University Press, 1989).

7 Kusmer, *Down and Out, On the Road*, 19.

8 Ibid.

9 Gross, "Giving in America."

10 Kusmer, *Down and Out, On the Road*, 21.

11 This, at least, is Kusmer's view.

12 Gross, "Giving in America," 39.

13 Franklin, "On the Price of Corn, and Management of the Poor," *London Chronicle*, November 29, 1766.

14 Wendy Gamber, "Antebellum Reform: Salvation, Self-Control, and Social Transformation," in Friedman and McGarvie, *Charity, Philanthropy, and Civility in American History*, 129.

15 Porterfield, "Protestant Missionaries," 61.

16 Alexis de Tocqueville, *Democracy in America* (New York: Knopf, 1994), vol. 2, book 2, chapter V.

17 Gamber, "Antebellum Reform," 129.

18 Ibid., 130.

19 Ibid., 131.

20 Gamber argues that antebellum moral crusades were not, as they are sometimes portrayed by scholars, simply a conspiracy by which white, middle-class citizens attempted to exert social control. For the fact is that many working-class and nonwhite citizens participated in these movements enthusiastically.

21 John C. Pinheiro, *Missionaries of Republicanism: A Religious History of the Mexican-American War* (New York: Oxford University Press, 2014), 1.

22 Ibid., 136.

23 Ibid., 17.

24 Ibid., 46.

25 Ibid., 48.

26 Ibid., 55.

27 Ibid., 33.

28 Kevin Starr, *Americans and the California Dream, 1850–1915* (New York: Oxford University Press, 1986), 93.

29 Maureen Fitzgerald, *Habits of Compassion: Irish Catholic Nuns and the Origins of New York's Welfare System, 1830–1920* (Urbana: University of Illinois Press, 2006), 86. This discussion of the child-saving movement and the Catholic reaction to it depends largely on this work.

30 Ibid., 88, emphasis in the resolution itself.

31 Ibid., 89–90.

32 Ibid., 97.

33 Peter Dobkin Hall, "The History of Religious Philanthropy in America," in *Faith and Philanthropy in America: Exploring the Role of Religion in America's Voluntary Sector*, ed. Robert Wuthnow, Virginia A. Hodgkinson, and associates (San Francisco: Jossey-Bass, 1990).

34 Stephen Warren, "Rethinking Assimilation," in Friedman and McGarvie, *Charity, Philanthropy, and Civility in American History*, 110.

35 Kusmer, *Down and Out, On the Road*, 26.

36 Gross, "Giving in America."

37 Ibid., 44.

38 Ibid., 45.

39 Kusmer, *Down and Out, On the Road*, 28.

40 Ibid., 28.

41 Ibid., 30.

42 Ibid., 30.

43 Walter A. McDougall, *Throes of Democracy: The American Civil War Era, 1829–1877* (New York: Harper, 2008), 565.

44 Kusmer, *Down and Out, On the Road*, 31.

45 Gross, "Giving in America," 47.

46 McDougall, *Throes of Democracy*, 590.

47 Ibid., 599.

48 Ibid.

49 Orestes Brownson, *Brownson's Quarterly Review*, January 1855, 48.

50 Ibid., 49.

51 Ibid., 193.

52 McDougall, *Throes of Democracy*, 605.

53 Ibid., 606.

Chapter 3

1 Quoted in Gustave Le Bon, *The Psychology of Socialism* (New York: Macmillan, 1899), 381. The first three sentences of this quotation were also chosen by Margaret Sanger to serve as an epigraph to her chapter titled "The Cruelty of Charity" in *The Pivot of Civilization* (New York: Brentano's, 1922).

2 T. J. Jackson Lears, *Rebirth of a Nation: The Making of Modern America, 1877–1920* (New York: HarperCollins, 2009), 13.

3 Ibid., 10.

4 Theodore Roosevelt, "Reform through Social Work: Some Forces That Tell for Decency in New York City," *McClure's Magazine*, March 1901, 448.

5 Lears, *Rebirth of a Nation*, 37.

6 See Benjamin Soskis, *The Problem of Charity in Industrial America, 1873–1915* (PhD diss., Columbia University, 2010), 51ff.

7 Quoted in S. A. Martin, review of *The Life of Charles Loring Brace,* by Charles Loring Brace, *Presbyterian and Reformed Review,* no. 24 (October 1895): 775.

8 See Soskis, *The Problem of Charity in Industrial America,* for a thorough and balanced discussion of this debate and many of the other topics discussed in this book.

9 Roosevelt, "Reform through Social Work," 448.

10 Ibid., 450, 451.

11 Jean Shepherd, ed., *The America of George Ade: Fables, Short Stories, Essays* (New York: G. P. Putnam's Sons, 1960).

12 This Ade fable is titled "The Fable of the Good Fairy with the Lorgnette, and Why She Got It Good" and is included in Shepherd, *The America of George Ade.*

13 Soskis, *The Problem of Charity in Industrial America,* 33.

14 *Homiletic Monthly and Catechist* 2, no. 10 (July 1902): 947–48.

15 *Homiletic Monthly and Catechist* 8 (1893): 38.

16 See, for example, Steven Pinker, "The Moral Instinct," *New York Times Magazine,* January 13, 2008.

17 Review of *The Service of Man: An Essay toward the Religion of the Future,* by James Cotter Morison, *Church Quarterly Review* 25, no. 50 (January 1888).

18 Dorothy M. Brown and Elizabeth McKeown, *The Poor Belong to Us: Catholic Charities and American Welfare* (Cambridge, MA: Harvard University Press, 1997), 3.

19 Ibid., 26, 28.

20 Ibid., 32–38.

21 See, for example, Pope Francis, "We Encounter the Living God through His Wounds," http://www.news.va/en/news/pope-at-mass-we-encounter-the-living-god-through-h; Pope Benedict XVI's encyclical letter *Caritas in Veritate,* issued on June 29, 2009, http://www.vatican.va/holy_father/benedict_xvi/encyclicals/documents/hf_ben-xvi_enc_20090629_caritas-in-veritate_en.html; and Benedict XVI's apostolic letter "On the Service of Charity," issued November 11, 2012, http://www.vatican.va/holy_father/benedict_xvi/motu_proprio/documents/hf_ben-xvi_motu-proprio_20121111_caritas_en.html, among many other examples.

22 Soskis, *The Problem of Charity in Industrial America,* 23.

23 Henry Ford, *My Life and Work* (Garden City, NY: Doubleday, 1922), 206.

24 Andrew Carnegie, "Wealth," *North American Review* 148, no. 391 (June 1889): 663.

25 Olivier Zunz, *Philanthropy in America: A History* (Princeton, NJ: Princeton University Press, 2012), 24.

26 Edwin Black, *War against the Weak: Eugenics and America's Campaign to Create a Master Race* (New York: Four Walls Eight Windows, 2003), xvi.

27 Ibid., 7.

28 Ibid., 13.

29 Quote in ibid., 18.

30 Sanger, *The Pivot of Civilization*, 108. Quoted in Black, *War against the Weak*, 129.

31 Black, *War against the Weak*, 28.

32 Ibid., 29.

33 Christine Rosen, *Preaching Eugenics: Religious Leaders and the American Eugenics Movement* (Oxford: Oxford University Press, 2004), 8.

34 Ibid., 14.

35 Ibid., 14.

36 Ibid., 17.

37 Ibid., 19.

38 Pius XI, encyclical letter *Casti Connubii*, issued on December 31, 1930, http://www.vatican.va/holy_father/pius_xi/encyclicals/documents/hf_p-xi_enc_31121930_casti-connubii_en.html; Leo XIII, encyclical letter *Rerum Novarum*, issued on May 15, 1891, http://www.vatican.va/holy_father/leo_xiii/encyclicals/documents/hf_l-xiii_enc_15051891_rerum-novarum_en.html.

39 Rosen, *Preaching Eugenics*, 26–29.

40 Ibid., 60.

41 Ibid., 81.

42 Ibid., 129.

43 Ibid., 122.

44 David T. Beito, *From Mutual Aid to the Welfare State: Fraternal Societies and Social Services, 1890–1967* (Chapel Hill: University of North Carolina Press, 2000), 2.

45 Ibid., 3.

46 Ibid., 28.

47 Ibid., 19.

48 Ibid., 49.

49 Ibid., 57.

50 Ibid., 224–26.

Chapter 4

1 Dorothy Day, *On Pilgrimage* (Grand Rapids, MI: William B. Eerdmans, 1999), 123.

2 This discussion of community foundations is indebted to Peter Dobkin Hall, "The Community Foundation in America, 1914–1987," in *Philanthropic Giving: Studies in Varieties and Goals*, ed. Richard Magat (New York: Oxford University Press, 1989).

3 See Kathleen D. McCarthy, "The Gospel of Wealth: American Giving in Theory and Practice," in Magat, *Philanthropic Giving.*

4 Peter Dobkin Hall, "The History of Religious Philanthropy in America," in *Faith and Philanthropy in America: Exploring the Role of Religion in America's Voluntary Sector*, ed. Robert Wuthnow, Virginia A. Hodgkinson, and associates (San Francisco: Jossey-Bass, 1990), 52.

5 T. J. Jackson Lears, *Rebirth of a Nation: The Making of Modern America, 1877–1920* (New York: HarperCollins, 2009), 45.

6 Mary Kingsbury Simkhovitch, *Here Is God's Plenty: Reflections on American Social Advance* (New York: Harper & Brothers, 1949), 100.

7 Ibid., 100.

8 Ibid., 102.

9 Ibid., 111.

10 Day, *On Pilgrimage*, 4.

11 Ibid., 20.

12 Ibid., 18.

13 Ibid., 23.

14 The 1968 number comes from Waldemar A. Nielsen, *The Big Foundations* (New York: Columbia University Press, 1972).

15 On these topics, see the many extraordinarily insightful philanthropic writings of William Schambra. Particularly relevant articles include "The Evaluation Wars," *Philanthropy*, May 14, 2003; "7 (Bad)

Habits of (In)Effective Foundations," *Chronicle of Philanthropy*, February 9, 2006; "James Q. Wilson and 'Broken Windows' Philanthropy," *Philanthropy Daily*, May 8, 2012; "The Problem of Strategic Philanthropy," *Nonprofit Quarterly*, August 12, 2013; and "The Tyranny of Success: Nonprofits and Metrics," *Nonprofit Quarterly*, December 30, 2013. These and other Schambra articles are available at http://www.hudson.org/experts/364-william-a-schambra.

16 James C. Scott, *Seeing Like a State: How Certain Schemes to Improve the Human Condition Have Failed* (New Haven, CT: Yale University Press, 1998), 89–90.

17 Ibid., 310.

18 Ibid., 332.

19 Ibid., 334.

20 Ibid., 196.

21 Dan Barber, *The Third Plate: Field Notes on the Future of Food* (New York: Penguin, 2014).

22 Wilhelm Röpke, *A Humane Economy: The Social Framework of the Free Market* (Wilmington, DE: ISI Books, 1998), 57.

23 Aleksandr Solzhenitysn, *Apricot Jam* (Berkeley, CA: Counterpoint, 2011), 21ff.

24 Leslie R. Crutchfield, John V. Kania, and Mark R. Kramer, *Do More than Give: The Six Practices of Donors Who Change the World* (Indianapolis: Jossey-Bass, 2011).

25 David Lapp and Amber Lapp, "Alone in the New America," *First Things*, February 2014, 31. I am indebted to the Lapps' article for the idea that human communion is what philanthrolocalism should ultimately be aiming to facilitate.

26 Thomas J. Tierney and Joel L. Fleishman, *Give Smart: Philanthropy That Gets Results* (New York: PublicAffairs, 2011).

27 Tachi Yamada, interview by Adam Bryant, "Talk to Me. I'll Turn Off My Phone," *New York Times*, February 27, 2010.

28 Anne Constable, "After 18 Years Leading McCune Foundation and Championing Causes around New Mexico, Owen Lopez Steps Aside," *New Mexican*, December 10, 2011.

29 Cf. Hunter's *To Change the World: The Irony, Tragedy, and Possibility of Christianity in the Late Modern World* (New York: Oxford University Press, 2010).

30 Shandra Martinez, "Grandchildren of Prominent West Michigan Donors Are Shaping the Future of Local Philanthropy," *Grand Rapids Press*, December 11, 2011.

31 Patrick J. Carr and Maria J. Kefalas, *Hollowing Out the Middle: The Rural Brain Drain and What It Means for America* (Boston: Beacon, 2009).

32 Richard Florida, *Who's Your City? How the Creative Economy Is Making Where to Live the Most Important Decision of Your Life* (New York: Basic Books, 2008).

33 See, for example, Christopher Lasch's *The Revolt of the Elites and the Betrayal of Democracy* (New York: W. W. Norton, 1995), and Bill Kauffman's *Dispatches from the Muckdog Gazette: A Mostly Affectionate Account of a Small Town's Fight to Survive* (New York: Henry Holt, 2003).

34 Kate Maternowski, "Small Towns, Big Scholarships," *Inside Higher Ed*, May 14, 2009.

35 Patrick Deneen, "Go Home, Young Person," *Front Porch Republic*, May 12, 2009.

36 Lapp and Lapp, "Alone in the New America," 31.

37 Private correspondence with foundation executive, who wishes to remain anonymous, December 7, 2013.

38 William Schambra, "Mesmerized by Metrics: Is Philanthropy Engaging in Magical Thinking?," *Nonprofit Quarterly*, January 27, 2012.

CPSIA information can be obtained at www.ICGtesting.com
Printed in the USA
BVOW08*1115300415

397544BV00001B/1/P

9 780812 247930